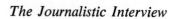

The Journalistic Interview

The
JOURNALISTIC INTERVIEW

REVISED EDITION

by Hugh C. Sherwood

HARPER & ROW, PUBLISHERS

New York, Evanston, San Francisco, London

STANDARD BOOK NUMBER: 06-013844-0

LIBRARY OF CONGRESS CATALOG CARD NUMBER: 72-79692

To Carli

Contents

Preface

When I graduated from the Columbia University School of Journalism more than two decades ago I was, I hope, a reasonably good writer. I think I also had some sense of what was news and what wasn't.

As I look back on it now, however, I was not a good interviewer. To some extent I realized this even then. Lack of experience and practice were, I suppose, the chief reasons.

Three of the next four years I spent in military service. Fortunately, my assignments were such that I was able to put much of what I had learned at Columbia to worthwhile use. I was even able to do some interviewing.

In any case, not too many months after my service had ended I had cocktails with a newfound friend—an older woman who had had experience in several facets of journalism. Among other things, she had written some cookbooks. And during a lull in the conversation I asked her how one went about writing a cookbook. One question led to another and, about 10 minutes later, she quietly told me I was an excellent interviewer.

I suppose there are a few times in every man's life when someone says just the right thing to him at just the right time. For me, that was one of those times.

This is not to say that I have not learned much about interviewing in subsequent years. I have learned a great deal. In fact, most of the precepts and some of the anecdotes in this book are based on this subsequent experience. To a lesser degree, I have drawn on casual professional conversations with fellow journalists and on occasional readings of what others have had to say about the art of interviewing, although, surprisingly, less has been written about it than you might think.

Nonetheless, I would be remiss if I did not give special thanks where special thanks is due. Two must go to Sterling M. Slappey and Bert H. Davis, both personal friends, for suggesting several of the better anecdotes in this book. Sterling is senior editor of *Nation's Business,* Bert a veteran business journalist who has himself authored several books. I must also thank Richard E. Mooney, another friend, for giving me the benefit of his thinking about off-the-record interviews, to supplement my own. These are discussed in Chapter 7. Dick has served in both the Washington and Paris bureaus of the *New York Times* and is presently the *Times'* assistant foreign editor. In addition, I wish to thank Wallace D. Huskonen, engineering editor of *Foundry* magazine, for allowing me to draw on his up-to-the-minute knowledge of the present state of development of the tape recorder, which is discussed in Chapter 5. Finally, I want to thank Mrs. Sandra Covello for typing the manuscript for both the original and revised editions of this book and, more important, for telling me that it was interesting. I hope you find it so, too.

White Plains, N.Y.   HUGH C. SHERWOOD

The Journalistic Interview

1.   Who Are You Anyway?

Someday, for the fun of it, stop a United States Marine on the street and ask him what his job is. Chances are seven out of 10 that he will answer "Rifleman."

It won't matter whether he commands a company, a platoon, or only himself. It won't matter that he may actually be a photographer, a cartographer, or a staff aide to the Commandant of the Marine Corps. Nor will it matter that a rifleman has the lowest, grubbiest, most dangerous job in the Marine Corps. The chances are still good that—be he corporal, captain, or colonel—the Marine will tell you that he's a rifleman.

The reason is simple. The Marines are trained to believe that their first, last, and most important job is to fight. They do most of their fighting on the ground. And on the ground the rifle is still this country's basic weapon.

The world of journalism is very wide. It includes newspapers, magazines, radio, television, public-opinion polling, public relations, and many subdivisions of all these functions.

Like the Marine Corps, it has its colonels, captains, and corporals. They merely bear such titles as editor or associate editor or columnist or director of public relations.

Whatever tasks these men actually perform, however, the best of them have never forgotten that their basic job is still the lowest—and the most important—in the field of journalism. They realize that that job is reporting. They know that, whatever their present tasks, they may be asked at any time to interview people, pore through records, and come up with a report that disseminates information that will be considered interesting, important, or useful—and, hopefully, all three.

Facts, information, knowledge reach these men, these reporters, in many ways. It may come through the pages of a competing publication. It may come through an annual report to a company's stockholders. It may come through encyclopedias or reference books. It may come through tips from friends or acquaintances. It may come through telephone calls. It may come through personal observation. It may come through press releases.

Yet the most important information they receive comes directly from other people. It comes through interviewing these people, face to face, for a few minutes or a few hours or even a few days.

Interviewing is no easy job. At its best it requires that the reporter make a careful choice of the person or persons he interviews so that he may obtain the most authoritative opinion possible on the subject at hand. In many cases it also requires that the reporter do careful advance reading on the subject he wants to talk about so that he will waste neither his own time nor that of the person he is interviewing, and so that he may go beyond basic, obvious questions and investigate the subject in depth. Obviously, it also requires a careful choice of questions, a careful listening to answers, a careful taking of notes, and a careful, objective report on what has been said and seen.

The best interviews usually take place in the office or the home of the man who is interviewed. Hopefully, that man has had several days' advance notice that he will be interviewed and some notion of what the reporter who will interview him wants to know. Hopefully, too, both the reporter and the man he interviews will have some time at their disposal—at least an hour, preferably two or three, possibly many more.

Not all interviews take place under such ideal conditions. Sometimes they must be conducted over lunch tables or in taxicabs or on street corners. Sometimes neither the reporter nor the person who is being interviewed has much, if any, advance word that the interview will take place. Sometimes the interview must be conducted in the space of a few minutes rather than in the space of a few hours.

Nonetheless, contrary to what you may think, the best reporter is not necessarily the man who can ask six or seven rapid-fire questions on the steps of a state capitol building or in the hallways of a court of justice, then run for the nearest telephone. Rather, it is the other way around.

The best reporter is usually the man who can ask 160 or 170 questions over the space of a few hours, then write a coherent, organized, interesting report on what he has learned. Hopefully, he will have several hours or days to do the job. But if not, he will be able to turn out his story on short notice.

Until he died a few years ago, the *New York Times* boasted one of this country's all-time great reporters. His name was Meyer Berger and, at one time or another, he covered almost every kind of story you could think of. In fact, the *Times* thought so highly of him that it assigned him to write its 100-year history, *The Story of The New York Times: 1851–1951.*

Berger hated the job. Although he did it brilliantly, he did it reluctantly. He longed to be back on the street, gathering stories for the daily newspaper.

Happily, one September day he was given a brief respite from his historical labors. A man named Howard Unruh had run amok in Camden, New Jersey, killing 12 people in only 20 minutes' time. Since most of its other ablest reporters were already out on assignment, the *Times* sent Berger.

I heard him tell once, in his diffident, almost halting way, how he had done the job. He had gone to Camden and interviewed almost everybody he could—police, people who had observed some of the killings, friends and relatives of the victims. He had even retraced the actual path the killer had taken and studied his war-souvenir-littered bedroom.

It took Berger many hours to gather the information he needed and, when he got back to the *Times* offices on New York's West 43rd Street, he had only 90 minutes to write his story. What he wrote took up all of one column on the *Times* front page and several more columns on an inside page—a total of several thousand words. It won him a Pulitzer Prize.

To gather his material Berger had to conduct many off-the-cuff interviews. But the man who would master the art of conducting this kind of interview will first master the art of conducting the long, involved, detailed interview. He will learn to ask many questions—both those that he has come prepared to ask and those that naturally occur to him during the course of the interview. He will learn to weed out the useful and important answers from the trivial and the irrelevant. He will learn to write a story that leaves no important questions unanswered in either his own or his readers' minds.

If he will learn to do these things and learn to do them well, then it will become second nature to him to conduct the quick, unexpected interview. By instinct he will know the 10 or 12 key questions he must ask. By instinct he will know whether he has enough interesting information for an article or not.

Whatever title you hold, whatever title you hope to hold in the world of journalism, you are then, first of all, a reporter. And to be a good reporter you must first of all be a good interviewer. Just how, you may wonder, can you become one?

Like men in every other profession, journalists have learned some techniques for making the most of an interview. Although these techniques are often simple, they are also effective.

For example, if a person fails to answer a question, it is often enough to ask him the question again. Or if he wants to answer a question off the record, it is sometimes enough to stop him in mid-sentence and tell him that you can get an on-the-record answer from another source.

I'll have more to say about techniques like these later on. What must be emphasized here is that no techniques, no tricks, no ploys will substitute for the impression you make as a person. Despite the thrill that some people feel at the prospect of being interviewed by a journalist, despite the suspicion, even hostility, that others exhibit, they will ultimately respond to you not as a journalist but as another human being. Make a good impression and, if the person whom you are interviewing is intelligent and informed about the subject at hand, you should get a good interview. Make a poor impression and you will fail—or at least come away with less than you might have.

How can you make a good impression? It's not very different from making a good impression in any other undertaking.

For one thing, you can be friendly. It's not necessary—it's usually not even wise—to meet the person you are going to interview with a beaming smile and a pumping handshake. Such exaggerated glad-handing may get you nowhere.

But a simple smile, a quick, firm handshake, and a direct gaze are called for. If I seem to mention the obvious, I do so with a purpose. Many people are just a little apprehensive at a first or even a second interview with a journalist and, therefore, just a little guarded. I have known this to be true even of people who have been highly successful and well known in their professions.

One reason isn't hard to guess at. Being interviewed is new to them. They want to make a good impression. And yet they're going up against something unknown to them—you and, more particularly, the questions you'll ask of them.

Then, too, journalism has had in its ranks people who have

given it, if not a bad name, then a poorer one than it should have. Most people have read about, heard about, or actually seen a hard-driving reporter who has virtually backed some poor individual against a wall and subjected him to a veritable third degree before letting him go.

In short, anything you can do to indicate to the person you are about to interview that you are friendly and well disposed will help you. If nothing else, it will put him at his ease. And that is the very first step to a successful interview.

For another thing, you can be intelligent. Unfortunately, but perhaps unavoidably, the person whom you interview may judge your intelligence in terms of your knowledge of his own trade or profession. If you know—or seem to know—something about it, he will be more apt to let down his guard and tell you things he might otherwise withhold.

Of course, being well informed about the profession of the person you are interviewing may not always be possible. You may be assigned to interview someone on a subject you know next to nothing about. Even so, you may be able to read up on the subject before the interview and familiarize yourself with it in a general way. You can at least remember the basic questions that must be asked in almost every interview. I refer, of course, to Rudyard Kipling's famous lines: "I keep six honest serving men/ (They taught me all I knew);/ Their names are What and Why and When/ And How and Where and Who." I refer, too, to such questions as: What are the benefits of this development (event, decision)? What are the drawbacks? What are the likely results?

Finally, you can avoid questions that deal merely with the trivial or the irrelevant. Show by your initial statement of purpose and your subsequent line of questioning that you are aiming at an intelligent goal, and you will inevitably draw the person you are interviewing along with you.

If it's important that you be friendly and intelligent when

you interview, it's also important that you avoid being a push-over for vague generalizations, evasions, and statements that are merely self-serving. There are, to be sure, times when it is wise to overlook a man's evasion or the self-serving nature of the information he gives you. This is certainly likely to be the case if he is, in general, providing excellent answers to your questions and if, furthermore, you have reason to believe that any attempt to bring him up short would end the interview or result in poorer answers to your further questions.

But cases like these are the exception rather than the rule. In general people are not impressed with journalists who seem callow, inexperienced, uninformed, easily put off—or too easily answered. Never let yourself appear in such a light.

A few years ago I had occasion to interview a man about profit sharing and other ways of providing people with compensation over and above their ordinary salaries. He was an intelligent man, well spoken, an expert in his field. But he was also an exponent of profit sharing, and I was not there to learn about the merits of profit sharing but to gain some basic factual information about it and to obtain an objective appraisal of it in relation to other methods of so-called incentive compensation. Before 10 or 12 minutes had passed, however, it became apparent that he was slanting his answers ever so slightly in favor of profit sharing.

I waited for his answers to another question or two, then asked him about a certain company that had suffered a strike as a direct result of its profit-sharing plan. Obviously, my question implied that profit sharing had drawbacks as well as advantages.

His face suddenly froze. He spread his hands palms down on the desk. And then, in an instant, he relaxed. His whole attitude changed. He began answering questions about profit sharing much more honestly and frankly than before, and he continued to do so throughout the interview.

I did not know as much about profit sharing as he did. I

still do not. But I had let him know, by a single question, that I knew more about it than he thought I did. As a result, a whole interview was changed.

Finally, if you are to be a successful interviewer, you must impress the people you interview as a decent human being as well as a good journalist. I know of no way you can accomplish this unless you treat them as human beings.

One way to do this is to treat them with reasonable courtesy. In our informal country, in an increasingly informal age, people very quickly get on a first-name basis. This, of course, has great advantages. But in many interviews it can be fatal to assume that you may address a man or a woman by his or her first name the very first moment you meet. In short, although it's wise to be relaxed and friendly, you will usually do well to let the person you are interviewing take the lead in putting your relationship on an informal basis. In the long run, I think, you will find that this approach will pay.

Another thing you can do is to show reasonable respect to the person you are interviewing. This does not mean that you should be deferential. In fact, if you are deferential, you will only put yourself at a disadvantage. The person you interview will assume that you think he is doing you a great favor in letting you interview him. He may even assume an attitude of noblesse oblige. The frankness and openness you had hoped for will disappear.

There are times in interviewing when it is necessary to be argumentative. There are even occasions when it is necessary to be rude. But these occasions are rare. If you will show reasonable respect to the person you interview, you will, in most cases, not be argumentative or rude, no matter how wild his person, his attitudes, or his opinions may seem to you. Rather, you will take down his remarks as faithfully as you can. And if you would impress him with your sense of responsibility, you may occasionally ask him to repeat a fact or a remark so that you can be sure you have taken it down correctly.

Yet even taking it down correctly will not be enough. You will also have to report it correctly. If this seems like superfluous advice, it isn't. Over the decades, a few reporters have deliberately misquoted the men and women they have interviewed or else have quoted them out of context.

Thus, one widely known Chicago public relations executive says he has been privy to a number of instances in which the press has deliberately set out to get a man. To do so, the journalists either misquoted the man or, more often, purposefully used only those quotes that supported their view of him or the view they wanted to present to the public. They have lacked the compassion, fairness, and objectivity that any journalist should have.

If you are a reporter, you must be an interviewer. And if you are to be a good interviewer, you must impress most of the people you interview as friendly, intelligent, not easily maneuvered—and, above all, as a human being who can be talked with as another human being and not just as a journalist.

The impressions you give cannot be faked. They must be part of you; for the very circumstances of your work will reveal many, many times whether they are part of you or not.

A few years ago I got to know a charming young man who had drifted out of law school and into journalism. After a few years of varied work, he had joined the staff of a magazine whose name is a household word in most American homes. He had not joined as a writer, but as a researcher whose reports would be used by other journalists as a basis for finished articles. He seemed to have a knack for gathering facts and, because of his relaxed, merry way, an even greater knack for establishing easy rapport with other people. In fact, he got them to tell him things that they did not seem to tell other journalists.

One day he was assigned to interview a nationally known woman singer and entertainer. The interview went swimmingly. In fact, after two or three hours of steady conversation she went so far as to confess to the young man that she was sexually frigid.

He asked a question or two, then went onto other matters. Not long afterward he ended the interview.

At three o'clock the following morning, he received a desperate telephone call from the woman. He would not, she asked, mention that she was sexually frigid, would he?

The young man said he would. The woman entertainer begged him not to and, when he balked, she pleaded—and even wept. But the young researcher was firm. She had given him the information. And he would report it.

The young man may well have been in the wrong. At least his editors seemed to think so. They had her confession on tape and could probably easily have withstood a libel suit. Nonetheless, they chose never to report her confession.

The point is not that the young man was wrong—or right. The point is that, if you ever interview any great number of people, you, too, will be tested as a human being. You will have the power to report—or not to report—their actions, their hopes, their fears, their frustrations, and their shames.

Sometimes you will be faced with requests to delete or change statements they have made to you. Sometimes you will be faced with requests to add to what they have said. Sometimes the requests will be trivial, irrelevant, or egotistical. Sometimes they will be weighty, pertinent, and modest. Sometimes they will be made matter-of-factly, sometimes plaintively, sometimes threateningly.

Sometimes it will not be an editor who will have the final say as to whether the request is honored. Because of lack of time, force of circumstance, or greater over-all knowledge of the situation you are writing about, the decision will lie with you.

And when it does, you will feel some of the power of the press and will sense that you hold part of that power. You will know that, to one person or to several persons or to a whole organization or even to a whole government, you are, for that moment in time, a very important man or woman. Just how important? That is a subject worth looking at more closely.

2. How Important Are You?

In England newspaper reporting is not a glamorous profession. The reporter is not looked up to, and he is often looked down on.

England, of course, is still class conscious, and the newspaper reporter does not usually wear an old school tie. Then, too, the English revere personal privacy to an extent that Americans do not, and the reporter is an actual or potential invader of that privacy.

Although much may be said against the status of the journalist in America, he is not looked down upon. And the bigger and better known the communications medium he represents—newspaper, magazine, or whatever—the more likely it is that he will be looked up to.

When all this began it is hard to say, but it may have been with the coming to power of President Franklin D. Roosevelt. Important, different, and exciting things began happening in Washington in those days, and the Roosevelt Administration was freer than its predecessors had been in telling the press what it was doing. Roosevelt was a master of the communications media, and he knew he needed the press to tell the American people where he wanted the country to go.

Furthermore, there arose in those days the great columnists—the semi-omniscient commentators on affairs great and small, who seemed to look on political events and administrations from a long way off and view them by the standards of the gods. Hard on their heels came some of the great World War II correspondents and then the television newscasters. The result is that, if you will ask today's American what he thinks of when he thinks of a journalist, he may be as apt to answer Eric Sevareid or Walter Cronkite or James Reston as he is the hard-bitten, hard-driving, hard-drinking newspaperman once made famous by Hollywood.

Journalism may not stand so great in the eyes of Americans as the law, medicine, or certain other callings, but it stands great enough. It is a glamorous profession, and it is likely to remain so for a long time to come. This glamour rubs off, to at least some degree, on all who practice it, and the closer one gets to New York City the more the glamour gleams.

Moving in this world of headlines and deadlines, of cables and microphones, it is easy enough to lose perspective. It is easy to become cynical. It is even easier to become self-important. It is easiest of all to forget that, no matter how well you speak or write, you are still only a conveyer of information, a catalyst, a middleman between sources of information and the vast reading or viewing public.

Yet this must not be forgotten. If it is, any one of several possible serious errors may result.

For one thing, the interviewer may forget one of the rarely voiced but cardinal rules of modern journalism. That is simply this: Almost all articles that appear in newspapers or magazines, and all reports that are purveyed over radio and television, are based on some authority. The authority may be a President of the United States or the head of some foreign land. He may be a medical specialist, a nuclear physicist, or a Broadway star. It does not matter who he is. What does matter is that his comments are, almost by definition, more important than how the interviewer reports those comments.

This is not to say that an interviewer should not strive to make his article or his story as interesting as he possibly can. It is to say that, regardless of how well written or spoken the article or story may be, there would have been no article or story if the person who was interviewed were not important, were not an authority in his field.

The interviewer who forgets this is liable to place himself first, his story second, and the person whom he interviews third. Such a subtle shift in attitude cannot help but be felt by the person being interviewed. And the interviewer who holds this attitude over a long period of time is bound to wind up with interviews that are considerably less successful than they might have been.

Yet this attitude abounds more than is commonly recognized. During the 1960 presidential campaign in particular— but both earlier and later as well—Richard M. Nixon was the victim of just such an attitude on the part of some of the American press. He was frequently subjected to overtly hostile questioning by various reporters who covered his campaign.

I do not wish to undermine what I am saying by giving the impression that I was a supporter of Nixon in 1960. In fact, I was not. Nor do I wish to leave the impression that Nixon was blameless. He may well not have been.

Nonetheless, newspapers and magazines themselves reported that Nixon was the subject of plainly unfriendly questioning— and of unfriendly stories. Some reporters had put themselves— that is, their own feelings toward Nixon and their own opinions of his political views—first, their stories second, Nixon third, and the American public last. Almost assuredly both the reporters and the public were losers.

A reporter for the Los Angeles *Times* became even more of a loser a few years ago when he let his temper get the best of him while interviewing the late Senator Robert F. Kennedy. The two were talking about the effects of television on presidential politics, and the reporter remarked, "Well, TV certainly is the fastest image-builder of any medium."

Turning on the reporter, Kennedy sharply retorted: "Don't use that worn-out phrase 'image-builder' on me. I don't know what you mean by 'image-builder.' "

The reporter, who was no admirer of Kennedy, became angry. He heatedly replied that the phrase was perfectly acceptable and that, if the Senator didn't know what it meant, everyone else did. Whereupon Kennedy turned on his heel and walked away, ending the interview.

The Senator had certainly been rude. But the reporter had even more certainly been unwise. He had let his real attitude toward Kennedy show through and, worse, he had lost his poise.

It is plain, then, that failure to remember that the person being interviewed is usually the most important aspect of a story is frequently compounded by another error: lack of objectivity. And this error can work both ways. Just as an interviewer can be subtly or overtly hostile to the source of his story, so can he be subtly or overtly too sympathetic or too enthusiastic. The results can be disastrous for responsible journalism.

Several years before he wrote *The Death of a President,* the contents of which the Kennedy family tried so hard to amend, William Manchester wrote another book about John F. Kennedy. It was called *Portrait of a President,* and it was extremely well written. But it was so blatantly laudatory and uncritical of Kennedy that it was sarcastically dismissed by more than one reviewer. It was plain that it would never hold a favored place in the annals of journalism, biography, or history.

Lack of objectivity can sometimes be an even more insidious danger if the interviewer talks with someone he does not know and about whom he has no preconceived opinions. The danger may be greatest with someone who is tremendously enthusiastic about his work. This kind of person usually makes the very best kind of person to interview. His eyes light up. The words roll off his tongue as he tells of his work with the gusto that only the truly dedicated professional can bring. Before the interviewer knows it, he may assess the man's work as much more important than it actually is.

What I am saying, then, is that no matter how casual and friendly the interviewer may be, he must maintain a certain objectivity, a certain inner detachment, about the person and subject he is writing about. Yet this is easier said than done.

We are all people before we are journalists or polltakers or public relations men. And we carry our prejudices with us. Some of them are part of the very warp and woof of our own profession.

Take the simple matter of the colorful statement. By instinct every journalist likes to interview the man who speaks vividly and memorably—who is, as the saying goes, eminently quotable. In fact, it is easy enough to assume that the man who does not speak in this manner is somehow less interesting and less important than the man who does.

Yet most journalists have found by practical experience that this is almost never so. The ability to phrase things felicitously or colorfully is a wonderful gift. But it should not be assumed that the man who has this gift necessarily has a wealth of information at his disposal or a wealth of sound ideas either. Nor should it be assumed that the man who phrases matters in an ordinary way does not have a great deal of importance to say.

As an interviewer you will inevitably be tempted to judge people inwardly in other ways, too. They may seem too aristocratic and formal or too casual and easygoing. They may seem of great importance or of little importance in the hierarchies of life. They may seem too this or too that.

What's more, the whole problem will be compounded by the fact that you will, by the very nature of your assignments, be compelled to judge the people you interview—at least in certain ways. Do they seem truthful? Objective? Knowledgeable? You will inevitably be making inward assessments on these and related matters during the course of your interviews—and afterward.

But resist the temptation to judge your interviewees as people, unless it is part of your assignment to judge them, for your attitude will inevitably creep into your interviewing and into the story you write, usually to both your detriment and that of your readers. Such subjective slanting can throw a whole article out of balance. And a sense of balance, a sense of proportion, in reporting on the affairs of the world is, in a sense, what journalism is all about—and what it needs a great deal more of.

If you do not agree, if you are an exponent of the so-called New Journalism, may I refer you to some very wise words from Eric Sevareid, the well-known television commentator: "We have all read the learned articles that tell us that objective news accounts in the hard news columns or broadcasts tend merely to deceive the reader or hearer, to obscure inner truths that the reporter perceives. He must therefore personalize the hard news, infuse it with his own truth. They would not leave this to the editorial writer, columnist, and commentator, whose work is clearly marked away from the hard news. They believe this will give a true integrity to news columns and news broadcasts. I believe it will ruin them.

"There is nothing new about this idea. In fact, this is the way it was done in the days of the Yellow Press and the screamers of radio's first, faltering years. This is the way it is still done in many countries. The result is that one must read many papers, hear many broadcasts, then try to piece together what really happened in any given occurrence. Inevitably, this becomes the journalism of polemics."

If a sense of balance and proportion is needed in interviewing people, so is it needed in assessing events and situations. Inevitably, of course, such assessments often derive at least in part from interviews.

David Hoffman, once a war correspondent for the Washington *Post,* recalls observing Joseph Alsop, the newspaper columnist, on one of the latter's trips to Vietnam. Alsop's hawkish views on the war are well known. So it's not surprising that Hoffman reports: "He worked his damned tail off. The damned hook is that, for all his work and sweat, he might just as well have been back home in Washington because he saw only what he wanted to see—just like the dove reporters, who also saw only the things they wanted to see."

Such lack of objectivity is a danger the good reporter always guards against. He must try to see and hear everything with fresh eyes and unbiased ears.

What I have been saying is that you must place yourself— your ego, your opinions, your feelings—last in an interview. You must place the person you are interviewing and the subject you are interviewing him about first.

If you do not believe that this is the wise course—or if you find it difficult to maintain an inward objectivity—give yourself a little test from time to time. Take some subject you know nothing about. Don't take nuclear physics or some subject most other people don't know much about either. Take a subject that many other people know a great deal about, but about which you know next to nothing.

Take cars. A great many American men know a great deal about cars. Some of them could even do a fair job of taking a car apart and putting it together again. Yet you might be at a total loss if you had to distinguish between a piston and a gasket.

Or take football. Most American men know a lot about the game. They know its lingo—safety blitzes, red-dogging, square-outs, and so forth—as well as they know the backs of their own hands. Again, you may know little.

But just suppose that you had to interview a top-flight mechanic on the chief differences between the cars of five years ago and those of today. Or suppose you had to interview a top-flight football coach on the differences in the way football is played today from the way it was played a decade ago. Who would be more important—you and your opinions of the man you interview or the man and his opinions about the subject at hand?

Perhaps you think I am pointing to a nonexistent danger. The fact is, it is a fundamental danger. It is part of the fact that you and I are human beings. Take this example: A few years ago a friend of mine was employed by a consulting firm. While he was away on a trip the firm decided that all its employees should be given psychological tests. When my friend returned to his office, another executive took him to lunch, presented him with a list of five companies that gave psychological tests, and told him to choose one—any one—and then arrange to take its test.

My friend chose three. "No, you don't understand," said the other executive. "You're supposed to choose only one."

"I will take three tests or none," my friend replied. "Here is what I am going to do. To the first psychological test I am going to wear a black suit, a black tie, and a black homburg. I am going to carry a black attaché case, and I am going to be smoking a black pipe. To the second psychological test I am going to wear a blue blazer, gray flannels, an ascot, and a sporty pocket handkerchief. And I am going to carry a cane. To the third interview I am going to wear corduroy trousers, a turtleneck sweater with egg spattered on the front of it, and a beat-up sport coat with elbow patches. I will obviously be in need of a haircut."

"But why?" the other executive asked. "I don't get it."

"It's quite simple," my friend replied. "The tests are obviously very similar, or you wouldn't have given me a choice of five tests. So the only thing that can differ is the psychologist who interprets those tests and his impression of me."

The upshot of the story was simple. The plan was reported to the highest level of the company, and a few days later my friend received a call from the president. The president quietly said that psychological testing had been canceled throughout the firm.

By now you may be thinking that you, the interviewer, are not at all important to the success of your interviews. Nothing could be further from the truth.

In fact, I think it is safe to say that, if an interview fails, the fault will be yours in 95 cases out of 100. There are instances, to be sure, in which people are by nature overly taciturn, in which they have not allotted enough time to be interviewed, or when for some other reason the interview fails through no fault of yours.

But these cases should be the exception rather than the rule. Provided you have chosen the person you are to interview with some care, provided you have familiarized yourself with the subject you are to talk about to at least a reasonable degree, and provided you have prepared your questions with precision, you should normally get a good interview, no matter whom you talk to. By good, I don't necessarily mean that a single interview will be sufficient for an article, although that may often be the case. I do mean that the interview will make a reasonable contribution to the total article or report you have to make.

How important are you? You are very important. Without you, there would be no interview at all. Without thought and preparation on your part, there would very likely not be a good interview. But you must view your role in perspective. You are basically conveying interesting information, important information, or both to an audience of readers or viewers. You are a catalyst, a person who draws out the opinions, the views, of another man or woman. The sooner your realization of this fact becomes an instinctive part of your approach the more successful your interviews will be.

One man who has rarely forgotten this is Dick Cavett, the television star. Strictly speaking, of course, Cavett is not a journalist. Nor do the interviews on his talk shows always resemble those conducted by journalists. Nonetheless, there are often sufficient similarities so that the wise journalist will take to heart one magazine columnist's recent comment about him:

"Cavett always asks the questions that are slowly forming, or should have formed, in the minds of his audience. He always allows the guest to respond. He follows and develops a conversation instead of driving it, like a dune buggy on an ego trip, into pit stops for a cheap laugh or a snide comment. His face reflects the intensity of the discussion, and he is not above looking honestly pained when a studio audience laughs at something morally outrageous. Yet his own disquietude never assumes the shape of a posture or a self-promotion. He doesn't weep or toady. He is there to let us see the faces and hear the voices of the men and women who have been out in reality, and whose scars of conscience glow in the dark."

3. *How to Get an Interview*

How do you get an interview? The answer to this question would seem simple enough. You ask personally, write to, or telephone the person whom you want to interview. You tell him who you are, what you want, and why you want it.

Often enough this simple answer is the correct one. And often enough it isn't. Sometimes, in fact, you'll be wise to approach the person you want to interview through a third party.

This is especially likely to be the case if you want to interview a businessman. In fact, you may take it as a rule of thumb that, if a company is big enough to have a public relations department, you'll probably be wise to work through it rather than approach the executive you want to interview directly.

It's part of a public relations executive's job to facilitate contact with the press. What's more, he's much more apt to perceive the value of publicity for his company than most other executives are.

For proof, some years ago I was assigned to write a story on how companies went about picking new presidents when they chose them from within their own ranks. It seemed logical to assume—and the assumption proved correct—that the men who had just served as presidents and who were now becoming

chairmen of their boards had played a major role in selecting their successors.

I decided to interview six presidents-turned-chairmen. But to get six interviews I had to approach 21 companies. What was wrong with the 15 companies that turned me down? In 13 instances the public relations director tentatively agreed to an interview, then was vetoed by his new chairman. Usually it was because the chairman was wary of offending men who had been passed over for the presidency.

The point isn't that many chairmen refused to be interviewed on this subject. The point is that many of their public relations directors thought they should be. The chairmen were wary of publicity. The public relations men weren't.

Naturally this isn't always the case. Much depends on the subject on which you want to hold an interview. Much depends on a particular company's policies and on its fortunes at a particular point in time. Much depends, too, on the kind of executive you want to talk with. Sales executives, for instance, are generally much more willing to be interviewed than treasurers and controllers. By nature and function the former are gregarious and outgoing. The latter are cautious and secretive.

In other words, you can sometimes obtain an interview with no trouble at all by approaching an executive directly. But, generally speaking, you'll do well to approach the men who are charged with obtaining publicity and goodwill for their firms—the public relations people. This rule holds particularly true when you want to talk with someone at a high level in a big firm. At a lower level in a smaller firm—even one with a public relations department—it's often a toss-up as to how best to proceed.

If going through established channels is often wise in business, it's even wiser in politics. During World War II the British Prime Minister, Winston Churchill, made frequent trips to Washington, D.C., to confer with President Franklin D. Roosevelt. Twice while Churchill was in Washington an editor I know was able to interview him on an exclusive basis. One of the interviews resulted in a story that produced headlines all over the world.

Did the editor approach Churchill directly? Obviously, it would have been extremely difficult to get at a man of his stature at any time. In wartime it would have been virtually impossible. Fortunately, the editor knew the British Ambassador to the United States, and the latter arranged the interviews with ease.

At lower political levels, too, the indirect approach is usually best. Senators and congressmen are busy men. If they aren't on the floor of Congress—and they often aren't—they may be out on the hustings making a speech or off in some foreign land conducting an investigation. Unless you're a Washington correspondent who is well known to them, you'll usually do best to approach their administrative assistants. This assumes that you want to talk with a senator or congressman at some length and not just ask him a few questions as he leaves the floor of Congress.

What's true in big business and in politics is even more true in the military. It's virtually impossible to get to see a high-ranking general or admiral at the Pentagon without going through a public information officer. And if you interview an officer of lower rank, what he tells you may have to be cleared through the public information office before it can be published. In general, the armed forces are stricter than most business firms have ever thought of being about who speaks to whom—and about what.

Out in the field, at the military posts around the country, things are a little less strict, but not much. Captains and colonels may sometimes be willing and able to talk about their posts' athletic teams or the morale of their men or the nature of the training these men are getting, without checking with higher authority. But they are unlikely to talk about anything meaty without making sure you have obtained clearance.

In combat zones resourceful reporters have sometimes been able to take officers or enlisted men aside and obtain a truer picture of the progress of a particular battle or the number of dead and wounded than any public information officer has been willing to give them. But these reporters have had to work with discretion, both for the sake of the men they interview and for their own. The military has ways of retaliating against reporters who go outside official channels, then write something it doesn't like.

Thus, in 1968, during the Vietnam War, a correspondent for the Baltimore *Sun* went to the battle area around Khesanh, which only a few months previously American troops had fought hard and successfully to hold. He saw that the Americans were abandoning the post and, believing that the enemy could see what was happening, he reported the abandonment in his newspaper.

In so doing he violated a ground rule for press coverage of the war. This rule stipulated that the press could not report movement of American troops without clearance from the military. This and some 15 other ground rules had been established by the armed forces in lieu of outright censorship.

As a result of his report, the correspondent lost his military accreditation card for two months and was put on probation for another four. This effectively prevented him from talking with either military or diplomatic officials, and it also barred him from using military transportation.

Indeed, the inherent tensions between government, particularly its military branches, and the press cannot be emphasized enough. The issue between them is almost always the public's right to know. The good reporter will probably have to deal with this issue sometime in his life, perhaps many times. If he wishes to keep working as a reporter and if he wishes to keep his sources of information open, he will operate with care.

Says Peter Arnett, a correspondent for the Associated Press who is considered by his colleagues as perhaps the best of all the reporters to have covered the Vietnam War: "Throughout the war, the Administration and the Saigon press corps have been natural enemies, like the cobra and the mongoose. We were attacked by officials because what we found in Vietnam was directly contrary to most of the ideas held in Washington. At times, particularly in 1966 and 1967, there was a conscious government campaign to discredit the press corps in Vietnam."

Adds Stewart Alsop, the well-known *Newsweek* columnist: "Anyone who has been around Washington for some time knows that a lot of governmental nonsense has been perpetrated in the name of security. Most reasonably diligent reporters, including this one, have been investigated by the government for publishing information the government found it inconvenient to have published."

In fact, the real attitude of many government officials toward journalists was neatly revealed in a memo written in 1963 by McGeorge Bundy. At the time, Bundy was a top-level adviser on national security to President Kennedy. And upon reading a press release put out by Pierre Salinger, Kennedy's press secretary, Bundy wrote him a note that read: "Pierre: Champion! Excellent prose. No surprise. 'A communiqué should say nothing in such a way as to feed the press without deceiving them.' "

Actors and actresses are more nonconformist than many other people. Besides, they are often located far from the organizations with which they are officially connected. Thus they may be appearing in plays on Broadway rather than working on a movie lot in Hollywood. For these two reasons they can sometimes be approached directly. Even so, they often have ties with studios or are represented by press agents. These organizations and people have a vested interest in getting their stars publicity. So here, too, it is often wise to work through established channels.

What about the millions of people who have no public relations executives, no administrative assistants, no public information officers, and no press agents? How do you get interviews with them? By approaching them directly.

It's getting easier to do, and it should get easier yet. The main reason is the rise of the on-the-spot television reporter. In recent years millions have watched these reporters roam among crowds after racial or other kinds of riots and ask questions of people sometimes picked at random. This kind of reporting has accustomed the TV viewers to seeing people just like themselves talk freely and naturally with reporters. As a result, I think, the future will find people less reluctant to become involved with the press.

Indeed, Charles Kuralt, who handles the On the Road features for CBS, reports: "People have been awfully good to us. I can't tell you the numbers of meals and the hundreds of cups of coffee we have been offered, and the hospitality with which we have been received. Part of the reason is that many people are used to seeing us on the air. So they are not surprised when we roll into town. In a way, they have been expecting us."

As I have indicated, the best interviews are ordinarily planned in advance. To get such an interview you must tell the person you want to interview who you are, with whom you're affiliated, what you want to talk about, how long the interview will take, and where it will be held.

Who you are is obvious enough. If you hold a high position in your organization, it's wise to make this plain. People who agree to be interviewed like to talk with someone who sounds important.

In telling what you want to talk about, be as specific as possible. Tell the person you approach not only the general subject you want to ask about but also, if possible, a few of the key questions you will pose. This should not only help you get the interview, but should also help the other party prepare to talk with you.

As a matter of fact, on occasion the other party may ask to see a list of questions you plan to ask, in advance of the interview. As a general rule, it's wise to cooperate with such a request. A more thoughtful interview may result.

If such a request is not made, you'll probably do as well not to offer to provide a list of questions in advance, unless you believe the interviewee will have to check his records in order to answer. After all, there's much to be said for obtaining a man or woman's spontaneous answers.

It's very important to make plain about how much time you'll want. Nothing can be more frustrating than to plan on a two-hour interview if the person you are interviewing has set aside only one hour. And this will often be the case with, say, a top business executive unless you have made plain your desires beforehand.

Just how much time should you ask for? There can be no flat answer to that question. Some reporters have conducted very successful interviews while taking a 10-minute taxicab ride with a governor or senator. Television reporters have sometimes been able to obtain significant statements in considerably less time than that.

Almost always, however, an interview of this length results in what is known as hard news—the kind of news that makes front-page newspaper stories. The newspaper or magazine reporter who must write a feature story obviously needs much more time.

Sometimes, in fact, an interview can run on for days. For example, an editor of *Playboy* once flew to Switzerland to interview John Kenneth Galbraith, the noted Harvard economist who served as ambassador to India. Galbraith was on a winter vacation in Gstaad, and the interview took up an hour or two of seven consecutive evenings.

Other reporters have been known to accompany celebrities for a day or even several days in order to get the kind of story they wanted. Obviously, to get this much time from anyone, you must represent a very well-known organization, and you must ask for the interview quite smoothly.

The typical interview should not last less than one hour or more than two and one-half hours. Especially if you want to interview someone on a subject of some substance, be reluctant to accept less than an hour—and certainly not less than 45 minutes. Otherwise you just will not have time to ask all the questions you will probably need to ask. And you will run the risk that the person you interview will just be getting warmed up when time runs out.

On the other hand, people usually run out of steam after two or two and one-half hours of continuous talking. So try not to ask for more, at any one sitting. In recent years I twice interviewed men for four hours. I had prepared carefully in advance, and the interviews went well. But at the end, both the interviewees and I were exhausted.

Deciding on where you will hold an interview is rarely difficult. In the vast majority of cases it will be understood that you will go to the office, home, hotel room, or whatever of the person you want to interview. It is simply a matter of courtesy that you go to the person you want to interview rather than ask him to come to see you.

Occasionally he may want to reverse this procedure. This may be the case if he is visiting the city in which your publication, studio, or station is located.

Wherever the interview is held, privacy is imperative. If you are visiting the person you are interviewing, then you must depend on him or her to prevent undue interruptions. If he is visiting you, the burden of privacy is on you. Nothing can do more to throw an interview off course than frequent interruptions.

So far, I have been talking primarily about what I would call routine interviews. By that, I mean interviews that prove relatively easy to obtain, regardless of whether one approaches the person to be interviewed directly or through some third party.

Obviously, however, not all interviews are easy to obtain. Sometimes they prove very nearly impossible. People who are in trouble—or who have friends and relatives in trouble—can often be as close-mouthed as a Vermont farmer. For example, in 1968, shortly after it was announced that James Earl Ray was wanted for the assassination of Dr. Martin Luther King, the black civil rights leader, reporters from *Life* fanned out through the Midwest in an effort to talk with anyone who had ever known Ray.

The chief of *Life*'s Chicago Bureau later reported: "The competition was terrific. We were always a step ahead of or behind the Los Angeles *Times* or the Federal Bureau of Investigation. Often doors were opened only once. When we were there first we got cooperation. When we were second we got nothing."

How do you persuade the mother or father of a murderer, or the relative or friend of someone else who has achieved notoriety, to talk with you? Often such persons don't need to be persuaded. If they do need persuasion, one strong argument is that the interest of their friend or relative will be better served if the public knows the truth about him, as they see it, than if the press is forced to rely on scratchy information or pure speculation.

Late in 1971, a New York reporter apparently used a somewhat similar approach to obtain a story from the assistant publisher of New Hampshire's Keene *Sentinel*. The publisher's son had deserted the U.S. Navy during the Vietnam War. Several years later he voluntarily returned to the United States to face the music. Although he refused to tell his story, his father told some of it for him. "Maybe it'll help him, and help us, and help a lot of other families who have gone through the same thing," the father explained.

In other cases, the resourceful reporter can often obtain what he wants by one or another of various stratagems. During the 1950s, for example, at a time when Sir Winston Churchill was still the British Prime Minister, an Associated Press reporter I know was stationed in London. He repeatedly tried to obtain interviews with Churchill. But so far from granting the reporter's requests, the grand old man didn't even bother to respond to his inquiries.

Finally, the reporter hit on a clever formula that he twice employed with great success. He framed just one or two pithy questions and mailed them to Churchill with a brief covering note. The note informed the Prime Minister that, unless he answered the questions in his next appearance in the House of Commons or in some similar fashion, the questions would be posed to him in person by a member of the opposition Labour party. Then the reporter looked up some member of the Labour party and got him to agree to ask the questions during the next Parliamentary debate.

Happily, the Labour party member never actually had to do the job. Churchill, who could be wily himself at times, fell for the ruse on both occasions. The reporter did not get a full-fledged interview, of course, but he at least got answers to the questions he considered most important.

Late in 1970, the chief of *Newsweek*'s Los Angeles bureau used a very imaginative method to obtain an interview with a member of one of the underground terrorist groups that were then beginning to prey on the land. Uncertain how to get in touch with such a group, the bureau chief simply placed an advertisement in a local underground newspaper.

Reading much like a nonstop telegram, the advertisement began: "To 'The Red Sun Tribe' or any other revolutionary anarchist group straight but hopefully honest writer for establishment but hopefully open-minded national news magazine anxious to explore mind and philosophy of bombers so as to be able to write article explaining what you're trying to say or accomplish. Absolute confidence guaranteed and will arrange meeting extent of what you want to reveal on your terms. . . ."

The advertisement soon produced a telephone call from a short, red-haired high school dropout who had served in the Vietnam War. The 19-year-old veteran, who identified himself only as Larry, agreed to meet *Newsweek's* man on a lonely strip of beach near Venice, California.

There followed a whole series of interviews that stretched over a week's time and took up, in the end, nearly 24 hours. Indeed, the bureau chief even persuaded the young veteran to take a tape recorder back to his terrorist group and record a statement from the group's leader.

The result of the interviews was a bone-chilling, five-column article that detailed the group's paramilitary training and maneuvers, plus its plans to try to take over the United States of America. The article began with the lad's threat to shoot police cruisers full of holes, "kill every pig on the street" and, indeed, blow up the whole world if necessary.

During World War II, a onetime newspaper editor named George Lyon served as deputy director of this country's Office of War Information and, as such, personally oversaw all news coverage of the European Theater of Operations. Lyon worked zealously on behalf of newspapermen, magazine writers, and radio broadcasters, who were often frustrated because top-ranking generals and admirals refused to talk with them. He soon learned, however, that formal complaints to these officers were of little avail.

So he occasionally resorted to a ploy that proved invaluable in getting cooperation. Because of his own high position in the Office of War Information, he himself was frequently able to see top-level officers. And he liked to get one of them alone in his quarters, pretend to be drunk, then roar, "Do you think the war is going to last forever?"

Once he had the startled officer's attention, he angrily announced that journalists were slow to forgive offense. After the war was over, he explained, they would be quick to let the American public know about excessive censorship and lack of cooperation on the part of the brass. The ploy usually worked, and the onetime editor got the cooperation he was seeking.

Take another example of how to get an interview when a direct, straightforward approach doesn't work. It involved use of a little honest blackmail on my part. But it got me an interview that I otherwise would not have obtained.

In 1969, many of the nation's brokerage houses sharply slashed the size of the commissions their stockbrokers could earn. The trend became so pronounced that, early in 1970, a spate of newspaper stories appeared, indicating that many brokers were considering forming or joining a union in order to bargain with their employers. The threat seemed serious enough so that several labor unions privately expressed interest in helping the brokers.

Whereupon a financial magazine assigned me to look into the prospects for unionization. I made a trip and a few telephone calls to Wall Street, then began placing calls all over the country—to Washington, Chicago, Detroit, and Los Angeles. I rapidly came to the conclusion, which ultimately proved correct, that the likelihood that the angry brokers would carry through their threat to unionize was slim and that, even if they did form or join a union, their chances of engaging in successful collective bargaining were not good.

Still and all, there remained an outside chance that the brokers would unionize. Much, it was obvious to me, depended on how their employers reacted to the threat. Unfortunately, on the advice of both their legal and public relations counsel, the top-level executives of most brokerage houses were turning a deaf ear to all pleas for comment.

Luckily, I reached the vice-president of personnel and administration of one of the best-known and most beleaguered brokerage houses in the country. Yet as soon as he learned what I wanted to talk with him about, he said he'd have to call me back later in the day.

He didn't call that day or the next. And when I telephoned him a second time, his secretary told me he was in conference.

A couple of more days went by, bringing me very close to my deadline. So I called the vice-president's secretary again and, after reminding her who I was, said something like this: "Would you mind giving your boss a message for me? Would you tell him that I have talked extensively with brokers and labor union leaders all over the country? I now know the brokers' side of the story. I also know the unions' side. And it is in the interest of your own company, plus that of brokerage houses generally, that I know management's side."

The secretary said she would pass the message on, and she was as good as her word. Two hours later, the vice-president called me back. He not only gave me a good interview, and one that helped confirm my original assessment of the situation, but he also pointed out an important aspect of the struggle that neither I nor apparently any other reporter had yet thought about. I wouldn't have obtained the interview at all, however, unless I had made a veiled threat to write a largely one-sided story because I had been denied access to the other side.

Sometimes, of course, a reporter can get an important interview simply by being in the right place at the right time. It may help, of course, if he or she also knows the right people.

Thus, in 1968, most of the world was surprised by the news

that Jacqueline Kennedy, widow of President John F. Kennedy, would marry Aristotle Onassis, the Greek shipping magnate. Nonetheless, a number of society reporters quickly flew to Athens, Greece, to cover the wedding.

Among them was Betty Beale, society columnist for the Washington *Star*. Miss Beale wasn't invited to the wedding. But she had been fortunate enough to obtain a hotel room on the same floor as Jacqueline Kennedy's mother, Mrs. Hugh D. Auchincloss. Mrs. Auchincloss spotted Miss Beale one day and promptly pulled her into her room to tell her about the ceremony. The interview lasted 30 minutes and proved to be the only exclusive prewedding interview with a member of the bridal family.

One of Miss Beale's competitors, Maxine Cheshire of the Washington *Post,* did just as well, although she had to do it in a much harder way. Instead of staying in Athens, Mrs. Cheshire went to a small fishing village opposite Skorpios, the island where the wedding took place. While there, she fractured her ankle scrambling over some rocks and had to go to a physician. They got to talking about the wedding, and he put her in touch with a local antique dealer who was one of the few non-family members who had been invited to attend. Mrs. Cheshire says the antique dealer told her all.

But if you want to study enterprise and quick-wittedness in obtaining hard-to-get interviews, consider one of the most famous interviews in the annals of American journalism. On Wednesday, February 15, 1950, a day that brought news of the signing of a 30-year alliance between Communist China and the Soviet Union, plus a plea by Winston Churchill for a top-level parley aimed at ending the atomic bomb race, the major story on the front page of the *New York Times* mentioned neither of these events. Rather, it was an exclusive interview that began:

"In the age of atomic energy, transmitted into a weapon

which can destroy great cities and the best works of civilization, and in the shadow of a hydrogen detonant which could multiply many times that agent of destruction, a serene President of the United States sits in the White House with undiminished confidence in the triumph of humanity's better nature and the progress of his own efforts to achieve abiding peace.

"This President, Harry S Truman, is a controversial figure in the world and in domestic politics. But to those who talk with him intimately about the problem of global life and death, his faith that these good things will happen, and probably in his own time, shines out with a luminous and simple quality which no event or misadventure of policy can diminish."

The interview, of course, was with the 33rd President of the United States. It covered many subjects—the so-called Cold War, deficit spending by the federal government, civil rights, and several others. It was conducted by Arthur Krock, then chief of the Washington Bureau of the *New York Times*. And it created an instant furor in the nation's capital.

A member of the House of Representatives went so far as to attach an amendment to a bill before Congress—an amendment that would have barred any President, any member of his Cabinet, or any head of a government department from granting exclusive interviews. Several members of the Washington press corps heatedly asked the President about the interview at his next press conference. And the President curtly told them to cool off.

Although presidential habits have since changed somewhat, up until that time Presidents of the United States had rarely given exclusive interviews. Woodrow Wilson had given a few. So had Truman himself—although never on such a broad scale or in the question-and-answer format that Krock had employed.

But these earlier interviews had definitely been exceptions. It had been a long-standing custom that, when a President spoke to the press, he spoke to all its members simultaneously. The press corps had come to rely on this custom, and it had been scooped.

As you can guess, the furor soon died down. Fifteen months later Krock was awarded a special mention by Columbia University in lieu of a Pulitzer Prize. The Pulitzer Prize advisory board made plain that he would have won the national reporting prize outright if he had not been a member of the advisory board and if it had not been the policy of the board not to give prizes to its own members. As it was, the committee did not give an award for national reporting that year, asserting that Krock's interview had been the "outstanding achievement" in the field.

As a matter of fact, Krock did not need another award. He had already won two Pulitzer Prizes for national reporting, one in 1935 and the other in 1938. Ironically, the second had also been for an exclusive interview—with President Franklin D. Roosevelt.

Did Krock obtain his exclusive interview with Harry S. Truman because he was one of the most distinguished journalists in Washington? Unquestionably. Did he also obtain it because he was connected with the country's, and perhaps the world's, most distinguished newspaper? Almost certainly.

But is it not also true that there were at least a few other distinguished newspapers in the land, with at least a few outstanding journalists on their staffs? Is it not clear, then, that, whatever Krock's prestige and affiliation, he got his interview because he had asked for it when no one else thought to?

Indeed, the origin of the interview couldn't have been simpler. Krock had been invited to a posh Washington dinner party, at which President Truman was the guest of honor. After dinner, the men and women separated for a while, and Krock found himself talking with Fred M. Vinson, then Chief Justice of the United States. Nodding in Truman's direction, Krock indicated that he would like to ask the President several questions. He said he thought they would shed a great deal of light on Truman's attitude toward the Presidency and certain complex issues before the public.

Looking right at the President and speaking just loudly enough for him to overhear, Vinson said, "Why don't you ask him?" Whereupon Truman walked over to the *Times* bureau chief and said, "Ask me whatever it is, and I'll give you a straight answer."

Krock coolly and quickly said that he needed privacy and plenty of time. And just as quickly, Truman told him to call the White House press secretary and make a date. The interview and its subsequent publication followed in a matter of days.

The lesson is plain: Enterprise has always paid off in journalism, and it always will. Go and do thou likewise.

4. How to Prepare for an Interview

If I could write only one chapter on the subject of interviewing, this would be that chapter. The reason is quite simple. Nothing is more important to the success of most interviews than advance preparation.

In some cases, of course, there is no opportunity to prepare in advance. Thus a newspaper reporter on general assignment may be hurriedly detailed to cover a major hotel fire. He will have no chance to check in advance on how many rooms the hotel has or on whether anyone of importance is staying there. Nor will he have time to prepare questions. He will have to work swiftly and surely after the fact, drawing on all his skills and experience so as to ask the right questions and ascertain the information he needs.

Even the newspaper reporter who specializes in some area like finance or state politics may not have much time to check on the background of a fast-breaking story or to formulate the most important questions to ask. He may have to draw on what knowledge he already has.

But the newspaperman who is writing a feature story, the magazine writer who is doing an article, the television reporter who is preparing a documentary, and the public relations executive who is ghostwriting a speech all have time to do their homework. Normally this homework can be broken into two parts—reading about the subject at hand and preparing questions to ask about it.

Very often the journalist is judged consciously or unconsciously—by his superiors and by his reading, listening, or viewing audience—on how well he does these two things. And he should be, for question asking can be an art in itself. As Voltaire said, "Judge a man by his questions rather than by his answers."

How should you prepare to ask questions? By first deciding what information you want to get. The more specific and clearcut you can make your objectives the better off you will be.

For example, if you were assigned to interview a former President of the United States who had been out of office for 10 years, several possibilities would present themselves. You could plan on doing a human interest story, concentrating on what the former President's hobbies were and how he was spending his retirement years. Or you could plan on asking him what he thought of his successors and their performance in office. Or you could ask his views about the nation or the world in general. Or you could ask his predictions for the future. Unless you were very lucky as to the amount of time you had been granted, you could not hope to cover all these possibilities adequately in a single interview.

Once you have decided the general subject you want to cover, you should make your goals even more specific, if at all possible. For example, in the case cited above, you might decide that, whatever else the interview covered, you must find out the former President's views on any tradition-breaking legislation recently enacted by the Congress.

Obviously, deciding on the nature of the interview you want to hold requires that you know something about the man you want to interview. How much needs to be known varies greatly.

Nonetheless, it is usually important to know something, for such knowledge may even affect the way you begin the interview.

Thus, a theater reporter for the *New York Times* has observed that conventional question-and-answer interviews will not always work—or at least work in full—with some of today's hippier young actors and actresses. Some of the actors just don't like the somewhat formal structure of a question-and-answer interview. As a result, some reporters now just browse around an actor's living room and wait for him to begin the interview by making some interesting observation. Or they make some wildly improbable remark in the hope that he will answer back.

It can often be quite easy to learn something about a person in advance of an interview. Has he written any books or articles or made any speeches about the subject you want to interview him about? If so, get hold of them. They can reduce by half both the time you need to prepare for the interview and the time you actually need for question asking. They can also help you ask better and more precise questions.

In addition, they may help you prepare the results of your interview more effectively. One retired journalist says that, by studying the articles and speeches that had been written by people he planned to interview, he became familiar with some of their favorite words and phrases. Then, when he conducted his interviews, he listened carefully to see if the interviewees actually employed these words and phrases in answering his questions. If so, he pointed up their characteristic terminology in his resulting articles. More than once, he says, he was commended by the people he had interviewed for quoting them in a form in which they could recognize themselves.

Is the person you are to interview listed in *Who's Who?* Have any other publications published articles on him? Check the *Reader's Guide to Periodical Literature* and similar sources. The information you glean may not only provide answers to some questions you had planned to pose but also suggest more fruitful areas for inquiry.

Be on the lookout, too, for any idiosyncrasies the person may have. Such idiosyncrasies may help you break the ice with celebrities.

Alex Haley, who has handled several of the long, front-of-the-magazine interviews in *Playboy,* reports that he once was assigned to interview the late Adlai Stevenson, the Democratic presidential candidate in both 1952 and 1956. In preparing for the interview, he learned that Stevenson had a passion for eating tomatoes. "I was prepared to sound like a horticulturist when I went into the interview," Haley says, "because this is the kind of thing that will reach through layers of problems in getting to a person."

Interestingly, when getting ready for an important interview, Haley doesn't hesitate to wine, dine, and buy flowers or perfume for the interviewee's secretary, especially if she's an older woman who has been in the man's employ for a number of years. He doesn't expect secretaries to spill state secrets. But he says they do know their bosses' quirks and can often tell how the latter can best be approached—what, in other words, makes them flow.

If it's usually important to know something about the person you plan to interview, it's also wise to know something about the environment in which he works or operates. The Columbia Broadcasting System indicated just how important this can be during the 1968 presidential primaries. It assigned its television reporters to cover geographical areas as well as candidates. Explained a CBS executive: "There are always two sides to a campaign—the candidate and the region he campaigns in. Each of our men is expected to know the history of the area he covers, its power sources and its issues, in order that he may accurately measure the impact of a candidate. A man who only follows a candidate can't do that."

If the person you want to interview is a businessman rather than a politician, then he may work for a publicly owned company. If so, it publishes an annual report for its stockholders. Get hold of the two most recent issues and read them. It won't be necessary to master them in every detail. But it will be wise to have a good idea of what product or service the company provides, of what its recent profit record is, and of what its future plans are. In fact, the annual report itself may suggest some questions. So, too, may other corporate publications, such as internal and external house organs.

If the person you want to interview is an actor, he may have appeared in several movies, television shows, or on- or off-Broadway plays. Newspapers and magazines have probably commented on his performances and perhaps interviewed him at earlier stages of his career as well. Thus a great deal of information may be at your disposal prior to the interview.

If the person you want to interview is a sports star, a wealth of statistics has been compiled on his performance on the playing field. No doubt his athletic skills became apparent early in life. As a result, there may be interesting reports about him dating back to his high school days.

It is sometimes easy to get information like this in advance of an interview, sometimes not so easy. It is sometimes important to gather a great deal of such information, sometimes not so important. You can easily waste a great deal of time in research like this. In particular, you can read too carefully material that is not especially pertinent to the subject at hand.

How much time you should spend on advance research depends on how much time you have, how important the man you want to interview is, what the particular subject you want to interview him about is, how important the resulting article is expected to be, and other obviously related factors. Walter Cronkite, the noted newscaster for the Columbia Broadcasting System, spent 40 hours of study before telecasting the flight of

Apollo 14 to the moon. And because he believes he can best remember what he commits to paper, he typed up a thick notebook of background material before he even flew to Cape Kennedy for the flight's countdown.

Cronkite was not preparing just for an interview, of course, and the telecast in question was more important than most articles, stories, or television documentaries. But his preparation is indicative of what some top-flight journalists do in advance of important assignments.

Ordinarily, of course, you probably will not have as much time as Cronkite had. So in general, it is safe to say that you should spend as much time on advance research as you possibly can but that, in so doing, you should work swiftly. Gather a lot of information, but eliminate quickly anything that is not relevant, and devote your attention to the rest.

As you do this, jot down the questions that occur to you. This will save you the trouble of going over all the material you have gathered a second time.

Then compile your questions in a logical order. Some editors or writers like to go into interviews with only a few key questions written down or even with all their questions in their heads. If this method works for them, who is to quarrel with it?

I prefer a much more comprehensive approach. I type out all the questions I plan to ask, in the order I plan to ask them.

It seems to me that this method has several advantages. First, it ensures that I will remember all the points I wish to cover. Second, it makes it easier to keep the interview on track. For what inevitably happens, in nine interviews out of 10, is simple enough to describe. The interviewee answers the first five or six questions in order. But when he is asked the seventh question he somehow manages to answer the 27th instead.

Then the problem immediately arises: Does the interviewer go on to the 28th question or does he go back to the eighth? There can be no easy answer to this problem. But if the interviewer has all his questions written out, it is much easier to skip back and forth with the interviewee, as he wishes, and then lead him forward again in orderly fashion. In short, most interviews become somewhat unstructured as they progress, and a written list of questions gives the interviewer a structure he can return to whenever he feels it necessary.

There is yet a third—and more subtle—reason for typing out your questions. It is plain proof to the person you are interviewing that you have given some thought and trouble to preparing the interview. If this is not the sincerest form of flattery, it is the next thing to it. It is also a subtle suggestion to the interviewee that, if you have devoted some thought to the questions you will ask, he should give some thought to the answers he will give.

If you want still another reason for preparing an interview in advance, remember that, if you don't know precisely what you want to ask, there is always the danger that you will run out of questions. This can be very embarrassing indeed.

No doubt you remember Spencer Tracy, the famous actor who won two Oscars and the plaudits of millions of movie fans. As an actor he often portrayed strong and good men. It was hard not to love him.

Yet in private life he could be somewhat crusty. In fact, he guarded his privacy like a bulldog and was particularly averse to giving interviews. On the few occasions when he did give them he proved very difficult to deal with.

One reporter found this out the hard way, when he made the mistake of asking Tracy what qualities make a woman attractive. The actor thought the question was silly, and he quickly rejoined, "Young man, I'll give you 30 seconds to think of another question." The reporter didn't have one ready, and he couldn't think of one off the top of his head. Whereupon the interview abruptly ended.

If you hope to present the results of an interview in question-and-answer form, I believe that it is almost mandatory that you write out your questions in advance. After the interview is over, for one reason or another, you may decide that you cannot write the article as you had planned. But if you have not approached the interview in a carefully structured fashion in the first place, I doubt very much that you will be able to turn it into a question-and-answer interview after the fact.

In preparing for an interview, remember to be very careful of the way you phrase your questions. Public-opinion pollsters have long known that the way questions are phrased can drastically affect the answers. As a result, they go to great pains to word their questions so as to avoid any show of partiality and so as to prevent people from feeling that they are expected to answer in a certain way. This kind of painstaking care can be very important, because some people are highly susceptible to influence.

The lesson is plain enough: Avoid asking leading questions. The less intelligent and educated the person you interview the more apt he will be to tell you what you want to hear, which may not be either the truth or his own real opinion. And the more intelligent and well educated the person the more apt he will be to see through your ploy—and to resent it.

Another lesson is: Be careful of what qualifying words you use. Words like "always," "never," "sometimes," "usually," "very," and so on can markedly affect the meaning of a question—and, of course, the answer you receive. You must use such words sometimes. In fact, it is often wise to use them. But use them with care and make sure the interviewee understands how they affect the meaning of a question.

It follows, of course, that another rule for preparing an interview is: Make sure your questions are very clear. In this connection, bear in mind that we almost all talk somewhat differently from the way we write. When we talk we are apt to be informal, to condense our statements, and to count on gestures to convey some of our meaning. So, if you draw up a list of written questions, remember that you will be tempted to phrase the questions just a little differently when you actually ask them.

There is a good way around this problem, however. When you write your questions down, pretend you are actually posing them to the person you are going to interview. With a little practice you will pick up the knack of rewriting and rephrasing the questions as you are apt to ask them.

Another way to ensure that your questions are clear is to make them as specific as possible. This is not always feasible, of course. Sometimes it is not even wise. If, say, you are dealing with a truly brilliant man, it is sometimes best to ask broad, general questions, then let him carry the ball.

Nonetheless, as a general rule, specific questions beget specific answers. General questions beget general—and often useless—answers.

Still another way to ensure clarity is to avoid asking several questions at once. Ask one question at a time, even if you have to break what is naturally a several-part question into two or three questions. If you don't follow this procedure, you will often create confusion and receive disorganized answers.

So may you create confusion, plus uncertainty about the validity of the answers you receive, if you pack too much information or a wealth of issues into a single question. Thus one of the nation's leading public-opinion pollsters recently posed this question to some 3,000 Americans: "It has been proposed that Congress pass a comprehensive health insurance program which would combine federal government, employer, and employee contributions into one health insurance system. Opponents say that would get the federal government too much into medicine and health care. Supporters say such insurance is necessary for people to obtain proper coverage. Do you favor or oppose such a comprehensive federal health insurance program?"

The pollster got responses to its question. And the resulting story produced at least one good newspaper headline. But it is far from certain that it produced good journalism. Anyone who has studied the various health insurance bills introduced into Congress over the past few years knows that they cannot be accurately or fairly summed up by saying that they call for combining federal government, employer, and employee contributions into one system. The proposals vary much more greatly than that. And anyone who has studied these proposals also knows that the arguments for and against national health insurance, especially in the many forms it has been proposed, are far more complex than the two sentences in the pollster's question would indicate. It would have been much more effective to have broken the question into several parts and elucidated the nature of the alternative proposals more clearly.

If concrete, specific questions, asked one at a time, usually produce good interviews, bear in mind that this approach can be overdone. It can result in a sort of staccato interview, in which the interviewee answers accurately but much too briefly.

So be prepared to include some open-end questions, both to relieve the monotony of a long string of specific questions and to draw out the interviewee. Such questions often begin: What do you think about . . . ? Or, What sort of factors do you think . . . ? Or, What do you mean by . . . ? One internationally known management consulting firm has found that these kinds of questions often do the most to put the interviewee in a reflective, thoughtful mood.

Be prepared, too, to ask questions that get past the head and into the heart of the person you are interviewing. This can be particularly important with, say, entertainers or other people in whom there is a great deal of public interest, especially if these people are still climbing the ladder to success.

For example, don't hesitate to ask such people what their motivations and drives are. What objectives do they still wish to attain that they have not yet attained? What inner tensions must they cope with? What outer forces or conflicts? Hopefully, questions like these will get you past superficial, external answers from the person you are interviewing and into his real being.

Always be ready to ask basic, fundamental questions. As indicated earlier, it is important to do your homework and to know something about the subject at hand and about the person you will talk with. But unless you are a specialist, it is often impossible to understand every facet of the subject at hand. So, unless you ask so many basic, elementary questions that the interviewee concludes that you are either an ignoramus or that you haven't done your homework, you cannot often go wrong by trying to clear up any points about his thinking or his profession that you don't understand. Most people who agree to be interviewed are willing to be helpful. Sometimes they are even pleased to assume the role of teacher.

There's another reason for being willing to ask basic questions. Sometimes you can obtain new and interesting insights into old problems. Thus I once had occasion to question several company presidents about the nature of leadership. Now, everyone knows what leadership is. But have you ever tried to define it—vividly and accurately and in only a few words? It's nowhere nearly so easy as you may think.

But two of the presidents got at the problem in a very interesting way—by telling me what leadership wasn't. As one of them put it: "Leadership is not mere drive. It is not merely the ability to get things done. Lots of men can get things done, but often these things have to be done their way and no one else's. As a result, they may be able to get a job done, but they may not be able to get other people to do it."

Take another example of the importance of being willing to ask basic questions—which, in some cases, may mean seeming to ask the obvious. As the story was related to me, a newly installed Secretary of State was holding his first press conference, and he was asked to comment on the basic purposes of the North Atlantic Treaty Organization. Whereupon he replied, briefly and rather testily, that the purposes of NATO were well known and that the new administration did not plan any changes in them.

When the conference was over, he exploded in private over the reporter's supposed stupidity and asked an aide who he was. Whereupon the aide was compelled to give him the name of one of the most famous newspapermen in the country. To top it all off, the next day the reporter's newspaper carried a front-page story to the effect that the new administration planned no major changes in our military and foreign policies in relation to Western Europe.

If you want further evidence that truly great journalists are not afraid to humble themselves in their own actual or assumed ignorance, consider this fascinating vignette of the late Henry Luce, founder of *Time, Life, Fortune,* and *Sports Illustrated.* The vignette is told by Gerald Holland, a former editor on *Sports Illustrated,* and it deals with a series of luncheons that were held prior to the founding of that magazine. At the time Luce was 55 years old, in good health, and at the height of his power and fame.

"The *Sports Illustrated* luncheons," reports Holland, "dealt in depth with a subject about which Luce was almost totally uninformed. He appeared to have given only passing attention to the sports stories in *Time* and *Life.* Now, because there was so much new to him, Luce took great delight in the luncheons. There seemed to be no end to the things to be learned and, like all instinctively good reporters, Luce never made a pretense of knowing something with the mental reservation to have someone explain it to him later. He grasped at everything he did not understand and pursued and probed it on the spot until he had it made perfectly clear to him. It was this unflagging, frequently uninterruptible curiosity, sometimes superficially comic, that was his hallmark as the last of the great founding journalists, the quality that made him to his last day more curious and inquiring than most of his writers and editors."

Remember the lesson then: A truly great reporter is not afraid to appear ignorant in order to get a worthwhile story.

One other bit of advice: Don't be afraid to ask tough questions, but don't ask dirty questions. By tough questions I mean questions that cause a man to think, to reflect, to search and, if necessary, to clear up any discrepancies in earlier statements he may have made on the same subject. To such questions you may not always get the kind of answers you seek. But if you ask six men the same tough question and five give you superficial answers, I think you will find that the sixth will often come through with a meaningful response.

But never ask dirty questions. By dirty questions I mean questions that are devoid of serious purpose and that are basically designed to embarrass the person you are interviewing—for no good reason. Dirty questions do no one any good, least of all the reputation of journalism.

Just a few years ago, a well-known television interviewer had occasion to interview a poet who was both blind and deaf. The poet had to place his fingers on the interviewer's lips in order to decipher her questions. And one newsweekly magazine reported that the whole affair had proved unusually moving, until the interviewer made the mistake of asking the poet if he missed going out with women. Then, said the magazine, it all became downright embarrassing.

Besides, if you persist in asking dirty questions, sooner or later you will get your comeuppance. Like the children of many famous men, those of Sir Winston Churchill had their problems and their ups and downs. As Randolph Spencer Churchill, Winston's only son, once put it, "When it is living under the shadow of a great oak tree, the sapling, so close to the parent tree, does not perhaps receive enough sunshine."

And yet Randolph Churchill apparently inherited enough of his father's flashing, devastating wit to put down any journalist. Once, while he was in this country, a television reporter asked him about his sister, Sarah, who had been arrested and fined for being drunk in public.

Snapped the younger Churchill: "I wouldn't think of asking you about your sisters. I was warned. They said, 'Don't you trust them. They'll spring something dirty, mean, or caddish on you.' I've not been disappointed—"

"Who told you not to trust us?" the television interviewer interrupted.

"I never reveal my sources of information," Churchill retorted. "I'm a journalist, not a television interviewer. I don't bother to look up what your sister has done or who your father was. I don't even know if you had a father or if you know who your father was."

If it's important to choose and phrase your questions with care, it's also important to present them in an organized manner. In listing your first few questions, bear two thoughts in mind. Don't start so slowly that your interviewee will quickly become bored. But at the same time start slowly enough—that is, in a sufficiently neutral vein—so that you don't intimidate him or give him the feeling that he can't cope with you. Thus your first three or four questions should usually be fairly easy to answer. Wait until the fourth or fifth before you begin to bore in on the subject at hand.

Of course, there are usually exceptions to every rule. When Jack Anderson, the widely known Washington columnist, wants to check a damaging bit of information with the person involved, he always begins by asking a question to which he already knows the answer. Then, if the man starts to give an answer that is not in accordance with the facts, Anderson says something like, "Now wait a minute. Court testimony indicates . . ." or, "I have a document that says . . ." He finds this approach usually throws the interviewee off stride and thus makes him more vulnerable to probing questions.

But an approach like this is useful only in special circumstances, as in investigative reporting. It is not likely to go over well with the ordinary interviewee, who may want to give you a good interview, and who may assume that you are a person of goodwill. Indeed, it may turn him off.

As for the rest of your questions, it should be easy enough to present them in good order. Just remember that the interview should move forward from one logical point to the next. The interviewee, to be sure, will probably jump about a bit. If so, you can more easily pick up the threads if your questions have been put into some logical pattern.

By organizing you can save both your own time and that of the person you are interviewing. And, as is the case with so many other things in life, how you use interviewing time can be all-important.

Although I have strongly stressed the importance of preparing for an interview in advance whenever you can, it is always possible that all your preparations will have been in vain and that you will have to deal with what amounts to total disaster. This can prove even worse than having to hold an interview on the spur of the moment, without any preparation at all, for the simple reason that preparation can cause one's mind to become overly fixed on certain specific purposes.

Such a disaster befell me not so long ago, for the first time in my life. I was assigned to interview the head of an important branch of the federal government, a man whose title would be instantly recognizable to almost every American.

The interview was supposed to begin at nine-thirty in the morning and last just an hour. But when I arrived, the number two man in the department's public information office rather curtly told me that the official's schedule had unexpectedly become clogged up—a not unusual occurrence in official Washington—and that the interview could last no more than 30 minutes.

Whereupon the number one man in the public information office briskly stepped forward, said he assumed I had a list of prepared questions, and asked to see it. Although his request was unusual, I reluctantly turned the list over. It ran to only 32 questions. And he ran down it rather quickly, marking x's or o's next to most of my queries.

An x, he explained, meant that the official would not discuss the question in point, either because it involved matters of policy that had not yet been resolved or because he was not empowered to answer without receiving permission from even higher authority. An o, he added, meant that the official could not respond to the question because he did not know the answer. He had been in office only 15 months.

When the public information officer got through, only five of the 32 questions on the list were unmarked. Although I had never been treated in this fashion before, either in or out of government, the public information officer seemed totally unconcerned. "Well, let's go upstairs," he said casually.

As we rode up in the elevator, I tried to maintain a conversation and also decide what to do. I didn't have much time to think, because I was very quickly introduced to the official I had come to interview. Although he was not an old man, it was readily apparent that he was a gentleman of the old school. And after just a very few moments of conversation, I said as quietly and as nicely as I could: "Your public information officer says you can answer hardly any of my questions. He doesn't seem to think you know much."

To this day, I'm not sure what word or phrase the public information officer muttered under his breath. But even if I did know, I doubt that it would bear repeating in these pages.

In any case, the official merely glanced at the public information officer out of the corner of his eye and smiled somewhat
thinly. Then he quietly began talking about a new development
in his department. Although this development bore no relation
to the questions I had come prepared to ask, it soon became
evident that he was giving me a scoop of rather major propor-
tions for the audience for which I was writing.

Almost needless to say, I changed my objectives to suit this
unexpected windfall. For the next 30 or 35 minutes, I had to
feel my way along in order to find out precisely what was involved.

I'd like to report that I asked every single question that I
should have asked, but I did fail to ask one that needed answering. Fortunately, I obtained the answer later in the day in a
conference with three lower-level officials who had been hast-
ily summoned by the chagrined public information officer. The
resulting article was the lead piece in the magazine for which I
was writing.

If I snatched success from the jaws of defeat, it was not because of any sudden inspiration on my part. It was because I
challenged an important official in as nice a way as I could
think of at the moment and remembered to ask the basic what-
why-when-how-where-and-who questions that must be asked,
somewhere along the line, in almost every interview.

In writing this chapter I have made two assumptions. The
first is that you know when to interview and when not to interview. The second is that you will pick your interviewees with
care. A word or two about both assumptions may be in order.

In general, the interview is most useful when it is employed
to obtain opinions—and opinions on matters of some signifi-
cance. It is much less useful when it is used primarily or ex-
clusively to obtain factual information.

There are two reasons for this. One, the written record is

a more reliable source of factual information than the human tongue. People often forget names, titles, figures, percentages, and all of the other precise data that can do so much to make an article or story or documentary seem—and be—well researched and factually accurate. What's more, although they may sometimes seem to remember such data, their memories may actually be in error. This can lead you into error yourself or cause you to undertake time-consuming cross-checking. Two, people will quickly become bored if most of your questions deal only with facts, and not with what they think about the facts. As a result, it's safe to say that you should never resort to an interview when you can get the needed information more quickly, more easily, and more reliably from a nonhuman source.

So far as picking interviewees with care goes, have some reason for approaching a man or woman for an interview. That reason can only be that there is some evidence that he or she can comment authoritatively on the subject you are investigating.

But picking interviewees with care means even more. It means knowing when to interview just one person and when to interview several—or many.

Occasionally this question can only be decided after you have completed one or two interviews. Perhaps the persons you have interviewed have not given you as much information as you had hoped, and you decide you must go elsewhere.

But it is usually best to decide on your number of interviewees in advance. You can go a long way toward making this decision by asking yourself two questions: First, how important is the first person you plan to interview? Is he so big, so famous, so in command of his field that his opinions in themselves are likely to form the basis for a solid story? Second, how broad is the subject you want to write about? Is it so broad, so subject to different approaches and different opinions, that no one man can be expected to have the final word on it or anything resembling the final word?

The answer to this latter question will sometimes be obvious. In other cases, answering it will require all the journalistic experience and intuition you can muster.

5. How to Record an Interview

Twenty-five years ago this chapter wouldn't have been written. Or, if it had been written, it would have been written differently. That's because there was really only one way to record an interview. That one way consisted of putting notes down on paper with pen or pencil.

Today this is no longer the case. Within recent years the portable tape recorder has made many recruits among journalists in all media. I do not know how many of them use tape recorders on a regular, as opposed to an occasional, basis, and I doubt that any figures are available. I would imagine, however, that such reporters are still in a very decided minority.

Even so, the tape recorder has made a splash. It's shown up at news conferences held by candidates for the United States Presidency and at interviews conducted with servicemen in bunkers in Vietnam. The Columbia University School of Journalism, the bellwether of America's journalism schools, now requires its students to gain some experience with the recorders. And at least one magazine editor says he considers his portable tape recorder as essential a part of his equipment as his typewriter.

In fact, the tape recorder has done more than make a splash.

In some cases it has enabled the talented, intelligent nonjournalist to compete on equal terms with the professional journalist.

Just a few years ago, for example, a professor of economics and finance at New York University's Graduate School of Business Administration traveled 75,000 miles throughout the United States and Canada, taping interviews with men who had played major league baseball during the first 20 years of this century. He let them reminisce not only about themselves but also about Ty Cobb, Christy Mathewson, and the other great stars of their era.

Then he wrote a book in which he recorded their memories almost exactly as they had spoken them into his tape recorder. The book was called *The Glory of Their Times,* and it was unquestionably a masterpiece of its kind. In fact, one big-city newspaper called it the best book ever written on baseball "any time, for any reason."

The many advantages of the portable tape recorder make it necessary to ask the question: Should the wise journalist use it, on a regular basis, instead of paper and pencil? Before discussing that question, I had better make three of my own biases plain:

First, I am a paper-and-pencil man. I have used the tape recorder in the past—rarely. I will use it in the future—rarely. By and large I will stick to note-taking.

Second, this does not mean that paper and pencil are inherently superior to the tape recorder. It merely means that they work best for me. For other journalists the opposite is true.

This is an important point. For the question is not how a journalist gets his stories, provided he gets them intelligently and ethically. The question is whether he gets them at all. In short, the wise journalist will use the tool that suits him best— and let the competition be damned.

Finally, whatever tool he uses on a regular basis, the good

journalist will have a sound working knowledge of both paper and pencil and the tape recorder. He will be able both to take good notes and to use a recorder—and be able to do so on short notice. The reason is that there are situations in which one tool is inherently superior to the other or even in which one must be used rather than the other.

For example, a member of the Washington press corps must know how to take notes, if for no other reason than that tape recorders are not permitted at the so-called background conferences sometimes held by the President, Cabinet officers, or other key officials of the federal government. Reporters who attend these conferences, which sometimes provide a great deal of useful information, are not allowed to attribute this information to the official who gives it but must credit it to "a high State Department official" or to "parties close to the President" or to some other unspecific source. Sometimes, in fact, the reporters are not allowed to attribute the information to anyone. It must seem to come from themselves and their general knowledge of the nation's political situation. In these latter cases, the conferences or interviews at which they obtain their information are known as *"deep* backgrounders."

Obviously, a tape recorder is not allowed at "backgrounders," because the officials who give them want to minimize the risk that their identities will be leaked—and proved. Reporters who attend these conferences observe the ground rules on pain of having their sources of information dry up in the future should they not observe the rules.

There are other situations where a tape recorder would not be welcome. Some people don't mind being quoted but don't want to be quoted quite so precisely as a tape recorder would allow. Other people—among them Norman Mailer, the novelist—complain that tape recorders destroy the mood and the intimacy that can build up between a journalist and the person he is interviewing.

For somewhat the same reason, R. D. Laing, the controversial British psychiatrist, once refused to let a writer for *The Atlantic* use a tape recorder. Explained Laing: "I don't want to make a public statement, to speak to all people at all times. The message I have to convey is from one person to another. I would rather speak to *you,* so that when you write something, it will be about *your* experience of me and of London."

Nor does the list of people who may not want their views tape recorded end here. Thus some people don't like what the tape recorder reveals about their ability to handle the English language. For example, I know of one company president who violently opposed use of a tape recorder in an upcoming interview. He had seen the transcript of an earlier tape-recorded interview he had given, and he had decided that his spoken use of the English language was not exactly eloquent.

Actually, the man was intelligent and well educated and had a good deal to say. But anyone who has ever read a few transcripts of tape-recorded interviews can sympathize with his viewpoint. In speaking the English language most of us get our syntax garbled, employ a few non sequiturs, fail to answer questions concisely and neatly, and in general reveal that we all write English better than we speak it.

Take the other side of the coin. There are instances in which tape recorders are, if not mandatory, almost so. This might well be the case if a journalist were about to write a biography of some living person or ghost an autobiography. In many such cases the journalist might interview the person involved for 20, 30, 50, possibly 100 or more hours—in, of course, suitable segments. And generally speaking, a journalist who interviews one person for 50 hours will do better to use a recorder than depend on his notes. When there is that much information to take down, the recorder will do a more thorough job than the human hand.

There are other instances in which a tape recorder can prove invaluable. If a reporter covers a conference where two or more speeches will be given simultaneously and where copies of these speeches will not be available, he can cover one speech in person and record another. Again, I have known rare instances in which people have said that they did not have time to grant a personal interview, but have told the reporters involved that, if the questions were forwarded by mail, they would tape their answers and mail the tape to the reporters.

Still and all, the typical journalist is not going to use a tape recorder two times out of three or paper and pencil two times out of three. He is going to use one tool or the other almost all of the time. So let's return to the original question—which tool should it be?—and look first at the advantages and disadvantages of the recorder.

The biggest advantage should be self-evident. The machine records—or should record—everything. This even the best of reporters, working with pencil and paper, cannot do. They can and should be able to record most things, especially all the main ideas of the persons they talk to. They may even capture *almost* everything. But unless an interview is very short and the person interviewed speaks very slowly, it is almost literally impossible for a reporter to take down every little word.

To this, of course, the experienced journalist may reply that it is rarely necessary to get down every little word. There are lots of words that aren't that important. And yet there are cases when it is desirable to do just that.

This might well be true if an interviewee were providing a journalist with a great deal of hard-to-understand technical material. It might also be true if an interviewee were to speak with a great deal of color or flavor, in a style all his own.

A few years ago, for instance, while holding an impromptu press conference, a Southern governor broke into a tirade against the federal government. Although the reporters present got down what he said, only one got it on tape. Yet when the governor had finished, all the other reporters turned to the man with the tape. "It wasn't so important what the governor said," the reporter later explained, "but how he said it—the rhythm, the lack of structure."

Just how well the tape recorder can capture the color of a man's language was nowhere better illustrated than in an interview that Israel Shenker, a reporter for the *New York Times,* held with the late Louis Armstrong just before the latter's 70th birthday. Any note-taker would have been hard put to get down all that the machine automatically recorded. Consider just these few paragraphs:

"In New Orleans," the great jazz musician said, "I played at as many funerals as I could get, and cats died like flies. So I got a lot of nice little gigs out of that. It's business. They're going to enjoy blowing over me, ain't they? Cats will be coming from California and everywhere else just to play.

"I don't know if they're going to be sad and when the time comes I ain't going to ask them, 'cause if I ask them somebody going to hurt themselves getting out of the way. I ain't going to ask nobody. I'm just going to keep my mouth shut. Yeah. If anybody plays a bad note, Lucille [Armstrong's wife] will slap 'em right in the face. She'll take care of that for me. I don't want no part of it. Once I cut out, forget it.

"It'll be good if I get to the Pearly Gate upstairs. Saint Peter will have all those good things written down. He ain't got no business with the bad things up there. Why should he tax me? We both in the same boat if we both up there. We all got a memory of some kind that was sort of devilish.

"When I go to the Gate, I'll play a duet with Gabriel. Yeah. We'll play *Sleepy Time Down South* and *Hello Dolly.* Then he can blow a couple that he's been playing up there all the time. He wants to be remembered for his music, just like I do."

All this is not to say that you should automatically turn to a tape recorder if you are going to interview someone known to speak colorfully. After all, Casey Stengel, the former manager of the New York Yankees and then the New York Mets, for years spoke to sportswriters in a lively, colorful, garbled kind of shorthand that could have driven the uninitiated up the walls. Yet many of these sportswriters got all—or enough—of Stengel's words down on paper so as to bring baseball's grand old man across clearly and interestingly to readers of newspaper sports pages. It is to say, however, that if you are going to interview someone who speaks colorfully, you might at least consider using a recorder.

You might do the same if you know you will be interviewing someone who is known to speak very rapidly. Governor Ronald Reagan of California does this, and some reporters who do not ordinarily use tape recorders have taken to doing so with him in order to make sure that they don't miss anything important that he might say.

A tape recorder can also protect journalists against charges that they have misquoted the person or persons they have interviewed. In a mayoralty campaign in Boston not long ago the reporters on one newspaper finally decided that they had to use tape recorders because one of the candidates kept charging that her views were being misreported. With tapes the reporters were able to prove that they had reported exactly what she had said.

In short, for a variety of reasons, it is sometimes good to have on tape a record of everything that was said. Yet the tape recorder offers other advantages or potential advantages as well. Some editors and reporters say that it enables them to relax and concentrate entirely on what they are asking and how an interviewee is responding, without having to worry about taking notes. Others say that a tape recorder can be particularly useful if they must interview a political candidate or anyone else in the midst of a noisy crowd. That's because they don't have to shove and push their way forward so that they are immediately adjacent to or in front of the man they are interviewing. They can be one or two men away from him and simply hold their microphones out. Often the microphones will pick up what the reporters can't hear.

Playboy interviewer Alex Haley once found himself in an unusual situation and his tape recorder of unusual advantage. He was interviewing the late Bishop James Pike, the controversial Episcopalian. The Bishop's son had recently committed suicide and, when Haley asked about it, the Bishop tightened up. So Haley turned away from this line of questioning.

But he came back to it a few minutes later when he changed reels. He merely said: "Now we should say something here about Jim Junior. The machine is on, so you just go ahead."

Suddenly realizing that he was out of cigarettes, he then excused himself and hurried to his car, leaving the recorder on. "I had started to run back," he recalls, "when I saw Pike from a distance, bent over the mike. He looked as if he were communing with it. And suddenly I realized that if you leave a person with a question and a recorder, after he is both used to the machine and to you, you'll get something from him that he perhaps wouldn't say to you or even to himself.

"I played back that section later on and was so moved by the way he went into that answer. He was feeling into himself. It was the kind of thing that came from his being, not his intellect."

There's one advantage of the tape recorder that is rarely mentioned—and perhaps rarely thought of. The recorder can enable a journalist not only to rehear the persons he interviews but also to rehear himself. This can be more important than you may think.

To some extent the success of an interview depends upon the rapport the interviewer effects with the interviewee. And by playing back a few tape-recorded interviews a journalist can learn a great deal about himself and the way he asks questions. He can learn in particular about his tone of voice. This is worth knowing, because often the tone in which a question is asked affects the answer that is given more than the question itself.

The reporter can also learn how well he phrases his questions —in particular, how his spoken phrasing of them compares with the way he has written them out in advance. He can find out how often he interrupts—and how he does so. He can find out if he is dominating interviews or if he is letting opportunities to ask questions pass by. In short, by playing back several tape-recorded interviews and by studying his style of interviewing a journalist may do much to make himself a better one.

I might add in passing that, if you do not habitually use a recorder, you can get some feel of how you sound when you interview people by employing a little trick recommended by speech coaches and often used by actors and radio announcers. Just bend one of your ears over and forward and hold it tight against your head. Then read several paragraphs of this or some other book aloud to yourself. In doing so, you will hear yourself exactly as other people hear you. And frankly, you may not be pleased. That, says one speech coach, is because most people speak several tones too high.

Before turning to the disadvantages of the tape recorder, there's one other point worth noting. Tape recorders are no longer the heavy, bulky, cumbersome pieces of equipment that they once were. Many are now light, compact, and easy to carry. For example, many so-called cassette tape recorders now weigh four pounds or less and can easily be slung over one's shoulder.

What's more, the cassettes now provide for two hours' worth of recording. This means that the interviewer can let the recorder run for one hour before turning over the reel.

To top it all off, the cassettes are not particularly expensive. Most of them range in price from about $30 to $170, and there is a sizable number to choose from.

All this is not to say that there are not other good portable tape recorders on the market. But one editor I know of with a particularly good working knowledge of tape recorders recommends the cassettes because of their portability, their good performance, and their general ease of use.

The greatest advantage of the tape recorder—its ability to record everything—is also its greatest disadvantage. That's because transcribing from a tape recorder takes a lot of time, more than many editorial offices can spare on a sustained basis. In fact, even listening to a tape takes a lot of time. Harrison Salisbury, an assistant managing editor of the *New York Times* with a Pulitzer Prize to his credit, says: "I rarely use the tape recorder, simply for mechanical reasons. You have to play the damn thing through, and that's like holding two interviews. I don't have that much time."

I know of any number of other editors and writers who don't use tape recorders, on a regular basis at least, for the very same reason. In the end this may well be the main reason why the tape recorder will never really supplant paper and pencil.

The tape recorder is also liable to pick up foreign sounds, and this can make it difficult for the interviewer or a secretary to hear what was said when the tape is played back. Air-conditioning machines can be particularly intrusive. So can the sound of a man tapping his fingernails on a table while he speaks. And so can background music. One trade magazine editor says he thought one of his earliest tape-recorded interviews had been a gem, until he played it back and found that Muzak had all but masked the interviewee's voice. Although the editor had hardly been aware of the music, his cartridge recorder had picked it up perfectly.

In addition, tape recorders often do not work well in a group interview. That's because the participants sometimes have a tendency to speak all at the same time, and this makes it virtually impossible for the transcriber to know what was said or who said it.

Then too, there's often a danger that a tape recorder will

dominate both the interviewer and interviewee. Says an assistant managing editor of a well-known business magazine: "When a tape recorder is used, both interviewers and interviewees tend to let it control the situation. The mechanics of the machine, the danger that it will break down, the interviewee's vanity all work against the interview. Somehow, the situation is no longer business—that is, facts and comments. Instead, it's show business. The interviewee wants to get everything just right and is overanxious to learn how he comes across."

Finally, there's the simple fact that tape recorders sometimes just don't work. Often the fault is human. Perhaps the interviewer forgets to turn the machine on or makes some other silly error that prevents it from recording. In other cases the error is not human. The machine or the tape breaks down.

This can happen to the very best of reporters and sometimes does. Early in 1970, James Reston, the noted columnist of the *New York Times,* held an interview with the late Gamal Abdel Nasser, then President of Egypt. Reston reported that he soon ran into "the inevitable tape recorder trouble" and had to wait patiently while two of Nasser's sons examined the machine and restored the sound.

I myself ran into tape recorder trouble once in an interview with a personnel executive in New York—and didn't know it. When I got back to the office and found that the interview hadn't been recorded, I rechecked the tape. I found that it had been torn during an interview held by another editor and subsequently spliced together with Scotch Tape. The machine had stopped recording the minute it had reached the Scotch Tape.

The possibility that a tape recorder will not record is worth remembering. There is hardly an editor or reporter of my acquaintance who has not suffered at least one fiasco with a tape recorder—and usually a total fiasco. Sometimes the editors have been embarrassed at their own oversights, sometimes outraged at the breakdown of the machine. In fact, I know of some journalists who are so aware of and wary of the possibility of machine failure that they always protect themselves by taking rough notes. To which the obvious comment is: If you think you must take notes, why use a tape recorder in the first place?

If journalists are outraged when a tape recorder fails to work, you can imagine how the people they have interviewed have sometimes felt. One of the worst cases I have heard about involved a very well-known U.S. senator. He was once interviewed for approximately two hours. Through an oversight on the part of the interviewer, the tape recorder failed to pick up a single word.

The interview was an important one. So the interviewer had to go back to the senator, confess what had happened, and ask for another chance. Almost needless to say, the senator was furious. The embarrassed editor got what he asked for, but the interview did not last anything like two hours. It lasted about 30 minutes.

All of which brings up the advantages and disadvantages of note-taking. They can be more easily recounted.

The biggest advantage of paper and pencil is speed. Not speed of recording. The tape recorder can record more rapidly than the moving pencil and, to varying degrees, depending on the skill of the journalist, somewhat more thoroughly, too. Nor does paper and pencil's advantage in speed involve just the fact that a reporter can work immediately from notes, whereas, if he uses a tape, he will have to wait for a transcript or else listen to a playback of his tape.

Paper and pencil boast another advantage involving speed. This rests in the fact that a reporter who has taken 10 pages of notes is in a much better position to go to work than a reporter who must work from 30 to 40 pages of transcript. Any journalist who has ever worked from a transcript and who has had to wade back and forth among the pages to find what was important—all the time disregarding digressions, non sequiturs, and the like—can attest to this fact. To put the matter in a single sentence, it is almost always much easier and swifter to write a story from notes than it is to write it from a transcript—counting from the time the transcript is ready.

In journalism speed is almost always important, sometimes all-important. So the journalist pondering how to handle a particular assignment must always give this factor weight. Often the weight will go against the tape recorder.

As already indicated, there are instances in which the tape recorder, if not banned outright, will not be welcome. It is rare indeed for a person to agree to be interviewed, then balk at having notes taken, unless he has so specified in advance. He may ask that certain individual remarks be kept confidential, but he is not apt to object to note-taking in general. But if a man agrees to be interviewed and finds that the interview will be tape recorded, he may agree to this only very reluctantly. Sometimes he will balk for reasons already indicated—e.g., an awareness that spoken words rarely read as well as written words—sometimes for other reasons.

Whatever the reason, when a person agrees only reluctantly to have an interview recorded, the whole course of the interview is likely to be affected. He may not give out information that he would have given out if the reporter had only taken notes. Or he may speak in a much more guarded manner, with the result that the reporter will obtain less than a true reflection of the man. In short, the interviewee who dislikes or is unfamiliar with tape recorders may not give as good an interview as would otherwise be the case.

This doesn't mean, of course, that there are not people who do like to have interviews taped. There are indeed such people. Some, in fact, are unduly flattered to have their remarks recorded. Nonetheless, there are many who feel just the opposite.

All this is a long way of saying that note-taking is almost

universally accepted in interviewing, while tape recording isn't. And the journalist who insists on using the recorder when it is not welcome may end up shortchanging himself and the organization he represents.

I'm sure that there are reporters whose pencil points have broken during interviews and who have had to take a moment out to borrow replacements from the persons they were interviewing. I'm sure there are reporters who have returned to their offices, only to find it difficult to decipher their own notes. I'm even sure there are reporters who have lost their notes (although I have never heard of any). Generally speaking, however, paper and pencil do not pose the problem of breakdown, through either human or mechanical failure, that the tape recorder does.

Finally, of course, paper and pencil are cheaper than the tape recorder. For a free-lance journalist, this advantage may be worth consideration. For the journalist employed by a magazine or a broadcasting system, however, it should not be a consideration—at least so far as the cost of the equipment goes. Even the smallest organization should be able to afford at least one tape recorder.

Yet the question of cost goes beyond the cost of the equipment. The time it takes a secretary to transcribe an interview can be very expensive, especially if such transcription takes place frequently. For just this reason one publication I know of allows—even encourages—its staff members to use tape recorders, but does not allow them to have the tapes transcribed. The editors must listen to the tapes themselves and, ironically, are often forced to take notes while the tapes are played back.

The major disadvantage of note-taking, of course, is that it can rarely record everything. And, as I've already indicated, there are occasions when it is important that just about everything be recorded. As a general rule, however, there is much to be said for the quick jibe of an old Associated Press reporter, "If you can't trust your notes in this game, then you'd better get out of it."

Note-taking is a part of journalism and almost certainly always will be. And the journalist who regularly uses a tape recorder because he thinks it can do a vastly better job of recording a conversation than he can is skating on very thin professional ice.

The assertion of some journalists that the tape recorder allows them to concentrate on asking questions and listening to answers without worrying about taking notes has merit. Interviewing with paper and pencil for any extended period of time does require intense concentration. The interviewer must ask questions, listen to answers, and take notes. He must also be alert to the necessity of probing into matters for which he has not prepared but which the interview itself makes plain must be looked into.

In short, interviewing by note-taking is hard work, requiring total alertness. But if a journalist knows his subject, has prepared for the interview in advance, and has mastered the art of note-taking, it is not as hard as all that. And it is something that any journalist is going to have to do many times in his career, no matter how often he uses a tape recorder.

To repeat what was said earlier, the wise journalist will know how both to take notes and to use a tape recorder. But for the journalist who prefers to use a recorder most of the time here are a few simple tips toward its more effective use:

First, know your machine. Know how it works. Know what it will do and know what it will not do. To begin to gain mastery over the machine, study its instruction manual thoroughly. Then practice with the machine for a while in the confines of your own office. Knowing your machine will not only enable you to get the most out of it but will also greatly reduce the chances that it will fail to record through an error or oversight on your part.

Second, whenever you are planning to use a recorder, take along more tape than you expect to use. The interview may turn out to be longer and more important than you had anticipated. How much more tape you should take along will depend on your circumstances, but possibly it should be twice as much as you think you will use.

Third, ask permission to tape record interviews. It isn't necessary to ask permission to take notes. But, for reasons given earlier, it is wise to ask if it's all right to record. If you run into a balky interviewee, tell him that you'll be glad to shut the machine off any time he wants to say something in confidence. Depending somewhat on the policies of the organization you work for, you may also be able to tell him that he will be given a chance to review the results of the interview prior to publication. And if it's true, of course, you can also tell him that you are not seeking sensational material nor trying to embarrass him or anyone else in any way.

Fourth, test your machine before the interview begins and at least once during the course of the interview itself. If you have time and opportunity to do the checking before the interviewee actually comes into the room, so much the better. If not, just turn the machine on and ask him to give his name, title, and affiliation. Then let him listen to the playback. Getting him interested in the mechanics of the machine is one way of relaxing him and establishing rapport.

Fifth, turn the machine off after you have tested it. Don't turn it back on until the man starts answering your questions or says something important. Interview transcripts or playbacks take long enough without burdening them with the preliminary remarks with which most such conversations usually begin.

Finally, never hesitate to turn off the machine if the interviewee begins to digress. One editor I know says he gets around the apparent insult by saying: "Excuse me. I am interested in what you are saying. But I have a limited amount of tape, and

I am going to cut the machine off for a moment." He swears the technique works—and often brings the interviewee back on course.

Also, of course, don't hesitate to turn the machine off if the interviewee receives a telephone call or someone steps into his office or living room.

What about the journalist who prefers note-taking? Here, advice is harder to give. For one thing, many journalists have evolved their own self-oriented techniques for taking notes. For another, I know from experience that they rarely think to exchange advice with their colleagues on this matter. Nevertheless, here are a few simple pointers:

First, learn how to abbreviate.

The reporters who are best equipped to take notes are those who have learned shorthand. But reporters like these are few and far between. I myself, in years past, once or twice considered taking a course in so-called Speedwriting, which I gather is a sort of poor man's shorthand. I never got around to doing so, but such courses may well have considerable value.

Without such a background, the good interviewer soon learns to develop his own informal shorthand. I have and, curious as it may sound, some of it varies from interview to interview, depending on the situation and my needs.

For example, I once had occasion to write an article on mutual funds, pension funds, and all the rest of the nation's so-called institutional investors. In order to write the article I had to interview several investment experts, and I knew in advance that they would all use the term "institutional investors" quite frequently. It's a big term to write out. So, in taking notes, I quickly abbreviated it to "ii."

There are all kinds of other possibilities. "Ind" can stand for "industry," "bus" for "business," and "gov" for the federal government. But these are only suggestions, and any journalist with a little imagination can work out the abbreviations that work best for him. He will need something along this order at some time or another—and usually many times—during the course of his career.

Second, learn to remember.

Any competent journalist gets down the high points of an interview. But often there is a great deal to write down—at great speed. So one thing I have learned to do is to listen so intently that I can remember whole anecdotes or vivid phrases for at least an hour or two afterward. When the interview is over, I write down these anecdotes or phrases.

This is a good way to supplement note-taking, especially when an interviewee is pouring out information or opinions very quickly. Experience leads me to believe, however, that a journalist must use this device sparingly and that he cannot plan its use in advance.

When he can use it depends largely on the person he is interviewing. Usually it's when a person speaks very forcefully, colorfully, and vividly—when, in other words, a person would normally be apt to remember precisely what was said, even if he were not holding an interview.

If you need help in improving your memory, consider playing a little game that one editor I know resorts to whenever he has to go into an interview without a tape recorder or, occasionally, without even paper or pencil. For 10 or 15 minutes, just before the interview takes place, he mentally spells difficult words backward. He says it takes only a few minutes of this to make him mentally alert and that he can then commit to memory much more easily whatever he can't write down.

This device may prove particularly useful to you if you ever have to interview a diplomat. The editor who conceived the game says diplomats are generally a dull, noncommittal lot and occasionally are deathly afraid not only of tape recorders but also of pads and pencils. This may be true, he adds, even when the interviews are off the record. As a result, he occasionally commits to memory everything the diplomats say. Then, when the interviews are over, he runs for the nearest hiding place and starts making notes as fast as he can.

Third, keep your pencil moving.

In almost every interview there come moments when the interviewee says things of little interest and moment. At such times it is only natural to be tempted to stop writing.

Never stop for long. The typical interviewee is apt to feel pleased that you have sought out his opinions. He is also apt to feel a little puzzled and perhaps slightly affronted if he notices that you are no longer writing his opinions down. And notice he almost certainly will.

Konrad Adenauer, the late Chancellor of West Germany, was known for observing the practices of journalists and for insisting that they take notes. Frequently, during the course of an interview, he'd turn to the journalist in question and say, "Here, take this down. Write it down." He was not only aware of his position and power, but he also wanted to make sure that the journalist quoted him correctly.

Besides, if an interviewee notices that you have stopped writing, his enthusiasm for the interview may begin to die. To avoid this happening, keep your pencil moving most of the time, even if you only scribble. He will never know the difference.

Fourth, don't worry about brief lulls in your question asking.

If an interviewee has anything at all of importance to say, he will sometimes get ahead of you. No matter how rapidly you write or how well you listen, you will still be taking notes when he has finished making a point. As a result, there will be a lull in the conversation before you ask your next question.

Unless these lulls are very frequent or last more than 15 or 20 seconds, don't let them worry you or throw you off your pace. The interviewee will usually be flattered that you are taking notes so assiduously. More important, a few lulls will give him time to collect his thoughts and perhaps add comments he otherwise wouldn't have thought of. In fact, once in a while I find that some of an interviewee's most pointed remarks come just at the end of such a brief lull, after he has had a moment to reflect on what he has just said.

Fifth, review your notes as soon after an interview as possible.

On this point all the journalists I've ever talked with about note-taking seem to agree. None of them put off the job of going over what they have written down.

If you can go over your notes almost immediately after an interview, so much the better. The conversation will still be fresh in your mind, and you can quickly fill in any gaps in your notes and write down anything tucked away in your memory. If you can't go over your notes at once, do so the same day or night. At the very outside, never delay beyond the following day. The human memory is more fallible than any of us like to think.

Sixth, don't depend on notes for long-term projects.

If you are going to use your notes the same day you take them, or the next day, or the next week, or within a month, fine. Especially if you take care to review the notes shortly after your interview, you should have no particular difficulty in transforming them into an article.

But if you are working on a long-term project and will be holding interviews over a period of many months, beware of relying on notes. Even if you review them shortly after an interview, you may find that, when you go to use them three or four months later, you will be somewhat at a loss. Words, phrases, figures, and anecdotes that might have seemed clear enough three or four days after an interview may not seem so clear now. In short, your interview may have diminished in value because you have forgotten most of the things your notes don't show and because the notes themselves, by their very nature, will not seem so clear.

I know of several journalists to whom this has happened. It happened to me once, too. Never again. I use my notes within a month of the time I take them—preferably sooner.

The moral would seem plain enough: If you don't think you will be getting at your notes soon, use a tape recorder. Or else, working from your notes, dictate a very detailed memo to yourself as soon after your interview as you can.

To sum up this chapter: In recording an interview, use the tool—tape recorder or pencil—that works best for you. But know how to use both. You never know when it will be either wise or necessary to employ the tool you don't habitually rely on.

6. How to Conduct an Interview

Not long ago a press release from an internationally known management consulting firm crossed my desk. The release dealt with a study the firm had made of interviewing and question asking. Among other things, it said that the success of an interview—any kind of interview—is determined during its first minute.

From time to time some preposterous statements are made on interviewing. But this is one of the most preposterous ever written. If it were true, I wonder how any of us would have enough courage to be interviewed for a new job, to ask for the hand of a woman in marriage, or to query a U.S. senator on his views on foreign policy. If it were true, we'd spend too much time worrying if our clothes were neat enough, our smiles broad enough, and our voices pleasant enough.

To be sure, it is incumbent upon an interviewer to do all that he reasonably can to set an interviewee at ease at the start of an interview. Basically, this means being pleasant and friendly.

But to say that the success or failure of an interview is determined in its first minute is little different from saying that the outcome of a football game is determined in its first minute.

Occasionally one is, of course—perhaps because the kickoff is run back for a touchdown and the opposing team is demoralized. But games like this are the exception. And so are interviews.

In fact, one rule for conducting successful interviews is not to dawdle over opening pleasantries. Although it is important to be reasonably cordial, it is also important not to waste much time on preliminary remarks, unless you expect to see the person you are interviewing a number of times. Often people are very busy and have taken time out of overloaded schedules to be interviewed. They may resent it if you seem to begin the interview by engaging in idle chit-chat.

The lesson is, get to the point. Rarely has this lesson been better illustrated than in an interview Booton Herndon held in 1968 with John S. Bugas, a former FBI agent who had risen to become industrial relations chief for the Ford Motor Company. Out of this and other interviews came Herndon's book *Ford: An Unconventional Biography of the Men and Their Times.* Herndon himself tells of the interview's beginning better than anyone else could describe it:

"My appointment had been made for me through the appropriate channels by the excellent public relations staff, and I had reported to Bugas's luxurious office exactly one minute before the time of the appointment. I knew that he had put in nine years with the FBI, and I've dealt with these types before.

"Bugas received me politely, if not warmly, gave me a firm handshake, and we sat down in the comfortable chairs around the oval table away from his desk. Tall, rangy and handsome, looking much younger than his 60 years, he made no response to the small talk I customarily use to grope my way into an interview. He just sat looking at me like a frog.

"I abandoned the small talk procedure and started on a nuts-and-bolts presentation of what I knew about his role in the rebirth of the company and what information I needed from him. I had my tape recorder with me, of course, ready to go, but I didn't touch it. When it appears that an interview is going to be difficult, I don't increase my chances of failure by fooling around with gadgets. I was desperately trying to elicit some spark of interest from his expressionless eyes when, suddenly, I found myself listening instead of talking. The transition was so abrupt that I honestly don't remember what it was I said that caused it. Whatever it was, I think it proved that I had done my homework and was prepared to listen intelligently.

"Bugas had been sizing me up. When he concluded that I was worth talking to, he did so."

As this anecdote indicates, one of the best ways to begin an interview is to remind the interviewee—very quickly—of the main subject of the interview and of the ground you want to cover. If he is the only person you plan to see, say so. He will attach more importance to the interview. If you plan to see other people as well, tell him so and tell him why further interviewing will be necessary. Then, in most instances, begin with a few interesting but low-key questions.

If it is important not to dawdle at the beginning of an interview, it is also important not to dawdle during the course of it. The typical interview lasts only an hour or two, and none of this time should be wasted. Besides, if you dawdle you run the risk that you will lose control of the interview or that it will lack direction.

An earlier chapter indicated that it can be important for an interviewer not to be afraid to ask basic questions—even to appear uninformed if the occasion demands it. It is also important for the interviewer not to try to be too clever. It almost goes without saying, of course, that he should pose intelligent, searching queries. But he should be straightforward about it and, unless circumstances are exceptional, avoid any attempt to put the interviewee on the defensive. Surreptitious attempts to pry information out of an interviewee or roundabout questioning are usually self-defeating. People respond to frankness and sincerity. They are on their guard when faced with someone who seems tricky or prone to show off his own knowledge.

As a matter of fact, of course, you will spend most of the time in an interview listening. Indeed, this is one of the most important things to know how to do—especially if you are taking notes at the same time. To do it well requires intense concentration.

Actually, the art of listening requires even more. If you would be really successful as an interviewer, you must learn to listen with the inner ear. You must hear more than the words the interviewee speaks. You must catch his hidden feelings, his unexpressed reactions.

In many ways this kind of listening is really watching. For you must observe the nods of the head, the winks of the eye, and the gestures of the hand that often tell more about the interviewee's true reactions than what he is saying.

As one student of interviews puts it: "You must get at what a man means, not just what he says. Much relevant information is communicated in a most oblique way. You must get at the 'hows' and 'whys' in order to reach your objectives. Probing is the key skill in interviewing. And in probing you may have to evaluate the degree of the interviewee's personal experience in relation to what he is saying."

How can you best probe? Ask open-end questions: What do you think about . . . ? Ask reflective questions: Can you tell me a bit more about how you feel . . . ? Ask interpretive or summary questions: You're saying then that . . . ? Or ask problem questions: Let's suppose that you're president of a company faced with the following situation . . . ?

Notice in the following brief excerpt from an article in an Italian publication how deftly the interviewer probes the views of the man he is talking with. He even argues with him, although never in an offensive manner. The interviewer is

Adriano Botta, an editor of *L'Europeo;* the man he is interviewing is Pietro Germi, the Italian film director. They are discussing Germi's film, *Chestnuts Are Good,* the story of a lovely girl who is determined to remain a virgin until she marries.

Germi: "Maybe I'm wrong, but I feel that my hero and heroine are not exceptional cases. For instance, I believe there are still girls who are virgins—and girls who still believe in simple and natural feelings, like Carla in my film."

Botta: "But is virginity so important?"

Germi: "No, of course it's not really important in itself. But it expresses a humble attitude of defense against the general breakdown of taboos."

Botta: "Still, the destruction of taboos can be a good thing."

Germi: "I have a great veneration for taboos. They are merely the expression of a moral law, which we have to have and cannot do without."

Botta: "Taboos hardly help us to live better. They're repressive."

Germi: "A moral code is always repressive. It says: This is good, that is bad. If progress and evolution have as their eventual goal a totally permissive society, then I am against them."

Botta: "But you who carry on so against eroticism gave the public a good dose of sex two years ago in your own film, *Serafino.*"

Germi: "But you misunderstand. I'm *not* against sex, so long as it's healthy. *Serafino* was a love story, told in a rather Boccaccio-like manner. What I am against is unhealthy eroticism. . . ."

As in this and other interviews, careful probing is important for another reason. No matter how carefully you prepare for an interview, questions will occur to you during its course that didn't occur beforehand. It is very important that you ask these questions at the time they occur, for they may affect the whole course of the interview.

Be especially alert to ask about anything you don't understand or that seems questionable. I know of more than one editor or writer who has been called out on strikes because he has let such opportunities pass by or because he has allowed an interviewee to slip a curve ball past him without swinging at it.

A few years ago, for example, a young editor I know was assigned to interview some businessmen who had entered politics. His task was to get their opinions on the advisability of other businessmen following their lead.

Although none of the men he interviewed was as well known as, say, Governor Nelson Rockefeller of New York, one had been a governor of a small New England state and another had been a candidate for governor of one of the major states on the Eastern seaboard. In short, the men the young editor interviewed were important men who knew what they were talking about.

He was scheduled to talk with six or eight such men, and his interviews were expected to extend over a period of several weeks. After a while a senior editor wanted to know how the younger man was doing. So he asked about the major disadvantages of businessmen going into politics. Without hesitation, the young editor replied, "The men I've talked with say there aren't any."

It was a ridiculous and revealing answer. For obviously a whole series of disadvantages would quickly come to almost anyone's mind. The cost of campaigning is one. The time campaigning takes is another. The possibility of being defeated is a third.

Despite these and other possibilities, the young editor had raised no objection when the men he interviewed said there were no disadvantages to a businessman's entering politics—presuming, of course, that he had asked about the disadvantages at all. I need hardly add, of course, that, because of these and other omissions, his article never quite came off.

More than once this book has emphasized the importance of being willing to ask tough questions, whether you have prepared them in advance or whether you must ask them on the spur of the moment. Nowhere was this need better illustrated than in a book that appeared a few years ago entitled *A Gift of Prophecy*.

As you may know, the book was about one Jeane Dixon, a Washington, D.C., housewife who is a so-called clairvoyant and who evidently has an amazing ability to predict what will happen in the future. For example, she apparently predicted the assassination of John F. Kennedy several years before he was even elected President.

A Gift of Prophecy was written by an experienced Washington political columnist named Ruth Montgomery, and it was both highly readable and highly interesting. Yet there was obviously something just a shade wrong with it. Perhaps it would be unfair to say that its attitude toward Mrs. Dixon was too adulatory. Nonetheless, without quite coming right out and saying so, it left the definite impression that Mrs. Dixon rarely erred in her predictions. This, despite the fact that she had erroneously predicted that World War III would break out in 1958; that Red China would be admitted to the United Nations in 1959; and that Charles de Gaulle would surrender his power as leader of France in 1964.

It was left to a well-known male magazine writer, Bill Davidson, writing in the *Ladies' Home Journal* some months later, to get at the truth of the matter. It was he who asked the tough questions: How often do Mrs. Dixon's predictions fail to come true? And when that happens, why don't they come true?

His examination of the lady's published predictions over a 12-year period indicated that only about 60 percent of them had proved accurate. Interviews with her friends indicated that, when her predictions failed to come true, it was usually for one of two reasons: either she had misinterpreted the symbols through which her foreknowledge comes, or else the people about whom she had made predictions had changed their plans.

It should be obvious that, when you ask tough questions, you may run up against a stone wall. The person you are interviewing may say, "I'd rather not answer that" or just "No comment."

Persistence can sometimes help greatly in coping with such a problem. If the question is a crucial one, you may be able to say that your editor will make you come back if you don't get an answer. Or you may point out that a refusal to answer may lead to rumor and speculation that could be even more damaging than the truth. Or you may threaten to obtain the answer from other sources—either the interviewee's friends or enemies.

Of course, there may be cases in which you have to accept a "No comment" and like it. This is perhaps most apt to happen if you are dealing with a U.S. Government official of some prominence.

For example, Ronald L. Ziegler, President Nixon's press secretary, often must refuse to comment on reporters' queries. But both Ziegler's associates and some White House reporters indicate that it is often possible to learn something from the very way he says "No comment" or otherwise turns questions aside.

In some instances, however, you may run up against more than an outright refusal to answer. You may run up against something resembling intimidation. That's what happened to Susan Sheehan, a staff writer for *The New Yorker,* when she interviewed Senator Edmund S. Muskie in late 1970. Here's how Miss Sheehan describes what occurred and how she handled it:

Muskie is as reluctant to talk about the United States' future role in Southeast Asia as he is now willing to talk about his past record on Vietnam. He knows where he wants to go, but he doesn't really want to talk about it. Questions provoke shouts and the old debaters' tricks of trying to turn the question on the questioner, both tactics calculated to intimidate the interviewer and evade an answer.

"You say you want to get out of Vietnam by the end of 1971, but are you willing to pay the price this might entail?" the interviewer, playing devil's advocate, asks. "Suppose the old domino theory has some validity and that our withdrawal from Vietnam causes the present Cambodian Government to collapse and we get an unfriendly government there. And suppose an unfriendly government comes to power in Laos or Thailand because we leave Vietnam and most of our influence on the Southeast Asia mainland goes by the board. Is this price acceptable to you?"

Senator Muskie scowls. "What the hell are you talking about?" he asks. . . . "What the hell are you talking about?" he repeats in a louder voice. He gets up and starts to pace back and forth across the room. "Do we have Southeast Asia to lose?" he shouts, whirling toward the interviewer. "Did we lose Red China?"

"No," the interviewer answers. "Chiang Kai-shek did."

"That's right," Muskie shouts, jabbing the air with his finger for emphasis. "So that's the answer."

"But it's not, Senator," the interviewer says. "My question is, 'Are you willing to give up American influence on the Southeast Asia mainland?' "

"Jesus," Muskie shouts, "you sound like John Foster Dulles with his pacts and all that nonsense. What influence are you talking about?"

"I'm talking about the governments in Vietnam and Cambodia and Laos and Thailand that are now friendly to the United States. I'm also talking about the air bases we have there. I'm talking about our physical presence. Are you willing to give all of this up?" the interviewer asks.

There is a pause. And then, at long last, the interviewer obtains her answer. Muskie begins it in what Miss Sheehan calls a parade-ground voice and ends it thoughtfully and quietly, sitting in a chair. It runs for several paragraphs, and it is both clear and to the point.

When you ask questions—especially tough questions—it can be important to check the answers that you receive. And this does not just mean checking factual answers with some outside source.

It can also mean checking the remarks of the person who is speaking to make sure you understand what he has meant. Probably the best way to do this is to repeat in your own words the gist of his remarks, then ask him if that is what he had in mind.

Checking the remarks of the person you are interviewing can also mean checking his authority to make them. Polltakers are prone to do this, and it is good that they do. For example, they may use what they call filter questions to ascertain an interviewee's knowledge of the subject at hand. Thus, if a polltaker is asking an interviewee about certain political matters, he may drop in some such question as: Do you happen to know the names of the two senators from your state?

Just how important it is to check the authority of people to speak on a given topic was well illustrated early in 1971, when Neal Sheehan, a reporter for the *New York Times,* reviewed a book for that paper's Sunday Book Review called *Conversations with Americans.* The book was authored by Mark Lane, a New York lawyer. Lane had conducted tape-recorded interviews with 32 veterans of the Vietnam War. And in the interviews, the veterans asserted that they personally knew of specific atrocities committed by Americans in Vietnam.

The book had already been favorably reviewed elsewhere, and Sheehan says his initial impression of it was favorable, too. But as a matter of routine, he checked the military records of some of the servicemen Lane had talked with, first with the Pentagon, then with other veterans. In a number of cases, he found the men Lane had conversed with had never received the training, belonged to the units, or been in the places they said they had.

Sheehan then called Lane and ascertained that the lawyer hadn't checked the veterans' stories either. Neither had Lane's well-known publisher, Simon & Schuster.

As Sheehan well observes: "It shocked me that such a sensitive subject hadn't been cross-checked. This is a basic thing you do if someone is making accusations against the credibility of an institution or of an individual." Indeed, but for Sheehan's own careful cross-checking, still another publication would have hailed *Conversations with Americans* as an accurate report of events said to have taken place in Vietnam.

Prepare in advance of an interview. Don't dawdle in getting started or in carrying through. Don't try to be too clever. Learn how to listen with more than common listening power. Don't let opportunities to ask key questions pass by. And don't fail to ask tough questions. All these are good rules for an interviewer to follow. But there is at least one other that is all-important: Never, never lose control of an interview.

An interview can go off the track for any one of several reasons. You may not have prepared in advance and may have no clear-cut purpose in mind. You may bore the interviewee by asking superficial, trivial questions. You may be up against an exuberant, dynamic personality who tends to seize control of things and talk only about those matters he wants to talk about. Or either you or the interviewee may get lost in some interesting but irrelevant digression.

It's usually easy enough to recognize when you've lost control of an interview. Either the interviewee is talking so much that you don't have a chance to ask questions. Or, if you are asking questions, you're not getting the kind of answers you want and need.

Not long ago, Nora Ephron mentioned such an experience in describing an interview she had held with Rod McKuen, the poet and composer, for *Esquire*. "It is not entirely easy to interview McKuen . . ." she wrote. "He tends to ramble. Ask him about his childhood and within seconds he will be off on a ramble about prejudice and the Army. Ask him whether his poetry paints too sanguine a picture of the world and before you know it he will be telling you about capital punishment."

Actually, failure to maintain control of an interview is not, to the best of my knowledge, a common problem. But it can crop up when you least want it to do so. And the worst of it is, the person with whom it's most likely to crop up may be one of your best subjects. This is the person who may have set aside a lot of time for the interview, who may be highly and visibly enthusiastic about his work, and who may be only too delighted to tell you all about it.

All this may sound wonderful. And, in fact, it often is. But there's a danger that a man (or woman) like this may get carried away with himself, may become involved in a talking marathon, and may tell you a lot of things that are interesting but irrelevant to what you want to write about.

The worst such case I have personally encountered involved a dentist who had invented a successful pain-killing device. I had asked him for an hour and a half of his time. And for a few minutes it seemed as if that would be more than enough. Although it was apparent that he was very busy, he was delighted to see me. I was able to ask only a couple of questions before he plunged into an enthusiastic description of his work.

In fact, he went on at such a rate that, during the next 40 minutes, I was able to ask only two or three more of the 40-odd questions I had prepared in advance. Soon I realized that time was running out. So I finally interrupted him and said something like this: "Doctor, everything you've told me is very interesting. But you've .answered only five of the 42 questions I came in with. I must get answers to the others if I'm to write a story. If you will just answer the questions I ask, I think we can wind up this interview fairly quickly."

It was, of course, a slap in the face. He flushed. But I had made the statement as pleasantly as I could, and it worked. The rest of the interview went off smoothly, and he was pleased with the story.

It's not often that an interviewer has to be this blunt. If an interviewee gets off the track, it is usually sufficient to repeat the original question or to go on to another one. But one way or another the interviewer must maintain control of the interview. In so doing he must walk a fine line between letting the interviewee have his head and following his own prepared list of questions too rigidly. If he goes too far in the first direction, the interview may never end. If he goes too far in the other, he may irritate his man and end up with an article that is lifeless and dry.

There is yet one other way in which an interview can become, if not precisely uncontrolled, at least unproductive. That is if the interviewee has a tendency to make broad, general statements without offering support for these statements. Unless the interviewee can speak with the authority of the Delphic oracle, such a tendency can be very damaging to the interview indeed. For it is anecdotes, examples, facts, and illustrations that bring most written material to life and that render any general observations an interviewee may make interesting and believable.

If the interviewee does not offer these in support of his observations, it is the duty of the interviewer to ask for, even to press for, them. It is not necessary, of course, that every statement an interviewee makes be supported by an example, but enough should be to make the result seem meaningful.

To every rule, such as never lose control of an interview, there are exceptions. They may be rare, but they do crop up.

A writer for *The Atlantic* ran into just such an exception not so long ago while preparing a story on Tennessee Williams. He visited the playwright at his home in Key West, Florida, for several days and saw a lot of him in his swimming pool, over cocktails, at dinner, and across the bridge table. But, he says, he soon found, "Nothing broke the flow of conversation quicker than a direct question." As a result, he had to leave it to Williams to bring up most of the things that were on his mind.

No reporter enjoys a situation like this, simply because the interviewee is in command of it. But such situations do occur now and then. And as *The Atlantic*'s writer learned, there is little one can do about it but adapt. It's important to add, however, that you should adapt only if you have plenty of time at your disposal. In a typical one- or two-hour interview you must press your questions home, in one fashion or another.

There is another possible problem in connection with conducting an interview. That involves knowing what to do if the interviewee lies. Actually, in my experience, lying is not a common problem. The interviewer may sometimes run across shadings of the truth or self-serving statements, but the outright lie is not frequent.

This, of course, is not to say that it does not occur at all. Some years ago, for example, I had occasion to interview a surgeon about a subject I have now forgotten. The magazine I was working for was also interested in the increasing number of malpractice suits to which doctors were then becoming subject. So I decided to question the surgeon about this and began by asking him if he himself had ever been involved in such a suit, knowing full well that a patient had filed one against him only a few weeks previously. His prompt answer to my question was: No.

It was one of those moments no one likes. I knew he had lied. And he knew that I knew.

Yet I did nothing. After a moment's hesitation, I passed on to another matter.

There can be no easy rule of thumb about what to do when a man lies. But if there were to be one, I would say that, in most cases, disregarding the lie is probably the wisest course. The reason is that, if you call the man's bluff, you will immediately put him on the defensive. And if, to use an old-fashioned term, he fancies himself a gentleman, he may be very embarrassed indeed. The rest of the interview is likely to be tense, awkward, and unproductive. Certainly the man who lies—and is caught at it—will not want to be interviewed by the same person again.

The determining factor as to whether to disregard a lie, however, must be the importance of the question and the answer to the story you plan to write. If they are central to it—or very nearly so—you may well want to make an issue of the lie, especially if you are sure of your facts. Whether you take issue adroitly or bluntly will have to depend on you, the interviewee, and the circumstances in which you are involved.

Even though outright lying may be infrequent, the experienced journalist soon develops a sixth sense about it. The sixth sense may not operate perfectly, but it operates well enough. The journalist usually recognizes when he is being lied to, even though he may not know what the truth of the matter is.

And if he does not know the truth, he can, of course, do nothing at the moment. In other words, to indicate or even to hint that a man has told a lie, when one does not know the truth, is the height of rashness. If you fall into this self-made trap, you may find yourself in the wrong, in which case you will be the one to suffer embarrassment. The better way is to probe into the suspected lie as deeply and as delicately as possible, then to check the matter later with one or more outside sources.

I might add that, if you are unsure of how to tell whether a person is lying, watch for these signs suggested by John Cronin, a well-known criminologist, who is an expert on interrogation methods: changes in posture, facial expression or tone of voice; redness of face; rigidity of body; dry lips, especially when accompanied by frequent wetting of the lips; plus overly terse answers to questions.

Cronin hastens to add, however, that these signs merely *may* indicate lying. They do not prove it. The interviewer must watch for other corroborative evidence, perhaps in the statements the interviewee makes or in information obtained outside the interview.

A far more subtle problem than the deliberate lie is the unconscious lie or distortion. It is also apt to be a more common problem and is, therefore, something every editor and reporter must be on the watch for.

One writer who ran into this problem not long ago was Donald Jackson of *Life*. His task was to prepare an article on what President Nixon was like as a young man. He soon found that nobody was neutral about Nixon, not even those people who had known him 40 years ago. He also found that everybody's memory of Nixon had been colored both by the passage of time and by his own current political viewpoint.

"I would ask a college classmate about Nixon's personality as a freshman football player," Jackson says, "and the classmate would talk about how determined Nixon was. Pretty soon he wasn't talking about the kid he knew 35 years ago but about the man he voted for two years ago.

"One woman I talked with had disliked Nixon when they were students together. She told me about a time she recalled seeing Nixon cheat during a college debate. He had been citing facts and figures from a piece of paper that was actually blank. After she told me the story she paused a few seconds and said, 'Gee, I *think* I remember that.' "

Unhappily, there was no easy way around this problem. Jackson says it took a lot of delicately worded questions and careful sifting of answers to obtain what he considered an honest portrait of Nixon as a young man.

All the while that you are interviewing someone you are forming some impression of him. Whatever the particulars of your impression may be, you are making an over-all estimate of him as a person—favorable or unfavorable.

If you are a wise interviewer, you will go into any interview with the secret assumption that you will like the person you are to interview. If you are even wiser, you will realize that it does not matter whether you like him or not. You are there to obtain a story, not to strike up a friendship.

Once in a while, however, you may run across someone whom you really feel inclined to dislike. In these cases it is important that you not show your true feelings. This can be easier said than done, of course, for most of us show our feelings more often than we realize. But showing them can set off a subtle reaction in the interviewee, who may secretly withdraw into himself or otherwise fail to provide you with all the material you would otherwise obtain.

There is a way around this problem, however. And that is to concentrate intensely on the subject at hand or on the article that you plan to write. Stop thinking of the interviewee as a person and regard him as what, in many ways, he primarily is —a provider of information or of opinions. Usually this will do the trick.

Few subjects have been written about less often than closing an interview. Yet closing an interview properly can be even more important than opening it properly. And for several reasons.

For one thing, you may someday want to interview the same person again, whether you realize that at the moment or not. Leaving him with a good impression of you is the best way to assure that he will be willing to see you again.

How can you do this? Don't allow the interview to run more than five or 10 minutes beyond the time you asked for. Of course, if you still have questions you'd like to ask and if the interviewee indicates, tacitly or overtly, that he'll be glad to continue the interview, that's fine.

But if he indicates he has other appointments, don't overstay your welcome. Try to arrange to return another day. Or ask if it will be all right if you call him up and complete the interview on the telephone.

Ordinarily, of course, this problem shouldn't arise. You should have foreseen your needs well enough to know, quite closely, how much time you will need. Whatever the situation, however, it is up to you to bring the interview to a close, barring any attempt by the interviewee to continue it.

Be sure to thank the person you've interviewed for his time and help. And unless he's really let you down, tell him the interview was good. Most people appreciate a brief word of praise about the interviews they give. I've even known presidents of well-known corporations to smile with appreciation when told that they had given an excellent interview.

The reason is simple. Most people have had very little experience with journalists. And at the end of an interview they like to think that they have done well, just as you would if you had undertaken a job with which you had had little experience.

If you know when the results of the interview will be published or otherwise used, say so. If not, tell the interviewee that you will let him know as soon as you can when they will appear.

Also assure him that you'll see to it that he receives a copy or copies. Making sure that he receives the finished product will do more to cement a relationship than any word of thanks or praise you may give.

By the time you have brought the interview to a close, thanked your man, praised him, and promised to let him see the final result, you may be getting up out of your chair or even going through the door. Your notebook will be closed or your tape recorder will be shut off.

Will the interview be over? Usually, yes, but sometimes, no. And the wise interviewer will be very alert to the possibility that it isn't over.

Why might it not be over? When an interview seems to have ended, any tension the interviewee may have felt may disappear. Or he may suddenly remember something he ought to have told you. Or he may let slip some revealing remark that throws the whole matter you have talked about into new perspective.

This kind of thing may not occur often, but when it does you may learn something of great value. It won't be necessary to whip out your notebook and take further notes. Just listen intently and remember what is said. Then write it down as soon as you can.

Whenever this kind of thing does happen, you can be sure of one thing: In the interviewee's eyes you have conducted a successful interview. For people do not pour out information after an interview is over unless they have decided that you deserve their help. And when they have decided that, you have indeed done well.

7. Three Special Problems

Not all interviews take place face to face. Not all involve only one person. Not all are published in a newspaper or magazine or reported through some other medium. For this reason I want to discuss three special kinds of interviews, all of which involve problems that do not usually occur in the course of the standard interview.

One of these special kinds of interviews is the telephone interview. The second is the group interview. The third is the off-the-record interview.

If a general rule were to be established about using the telephone to interview other people, the best rule would probably be: All other things being equal, don't do it. In most cases the telephone interview is simply less productive than the face-to-face interview.

It is no accident that almost all of the top public-opinion pollsters in this country prefer to conduct interviews in people's homes—or at least on their doorsteps—rather than by telephone. The pollsters believe that their interviewers can establish more effective rapport with people when talking to them in person rather than over the telephone. And they are right.

In a face-to-face interview the interviewer can be friendlier than on the telephone. He can more readily ascertain how the interviewee is reacting to his questioning. And he can more easily determine the interviewee's meaning by observing his facial expressions and his gestures.

If it is better from the interviewer's standpoint to conduct an interview in person, so is it better from the interviewee's standpoint. If you interview a man by telephone, he isn't able to see you any more than you can see him. In fact, he may not know either you or the organization you represent. For these reasons he may be more reserved in his remarks than would otherwise be the case. And he may be more inclined to terminate the conversation at the earliest opportunity.

It is important to bear in mind that the telephone is an intruder. Your call will come at a time when the interviewee does not expect it. He may be in the middle of an unusually busy day. He may not want to talk with you at all. It will not be as if he had set aside a special time and a special day to hold the interview.

There are still other drawbacks to the telephone interview.

There is a much greater danger that the interview will be superficial and touch only on the highlights of the matter under discussion. This is primarily because the telephone interview tends to be much shorter than the face-to-face interview.

It is also much more difficult to take notes during a telephone interview. You must hold the telephone in one hand and scribble with the other. Usually it is necessary to scribble as fast as you can. The interviewee can't see you doing this, of course, and any pauses in your conversation may seem awkward and strange to him.

Finally, if you want pictures to accompany the story you are planning to write, you will be at the interviewee's mercy, and that is the mercy of an amateur. If he must have pictures taken, you will have to trust his judgment as to what should be photographed and what should not. If he already has pictures on hand, you can only hope that they are what you are looking for.

All of which brings us back to the general rule: All other things being equal, don't use the telephone to interview people. And it doesn't take any reflection at all, of course, to realize that all other things are rarely equal.

So it's no surprise that editors, writers, and reporters constantly use the telephone to conduct interviews. They do so for all kinds of reasons. They may not have the time to give to or to set up a face-to-face interview; they may need information almost immediately. The organizations they work for may not have the money to send them 500 or 1,500 miles for an interview. They may just not want to make the effort. Or they may have only a relatively few questions to ask and may think—rightly or wrongly—that they can adequately cover these questions by telephone.

In short, the telephone is a very important and useful tool in modern journalism. So here are some suggestions on how to decide whether you should resort to it rather than to the face-to-face interview. The suggestions presume, of course, that you have a choice—that neither the pressure of deadlines nor the expense of travel effectively prevents you from even considering a face-to-face interview.

1. How many questions do you need to ask? If you plan to ask more than about eight or 10, in most cases it will be wise to see the party in person. The nature of interviewing itself suggests that a few additional questions may crop up during the course of the conversation. And more than is the case in face-to-face interviewing, people get tired during extended telephone conversations. As a general rule, the longer the conversations go on the less productive they are likely to be.

To look at the whole matter another way, if you think your conversation will last more than 15 minutes, give serious consideration to seeing the interviewee in person. In point of fact, the conversation will probably last 25 or 30 minutes. And that's long enough for any telephone interview to last, not only from the interviewee's standpoint but also from your own. Telephone interviewing is tiring for the interviewer, too.

2. How long and how important is the article you plan to write? The shorter the article the more likely it is to lend itself to telephone interviewing. If it will run to only two or three typewritten pages, you may easily be able to find out all you need to know by telephone. If it will run to 10 or 12 pages, however, it is very doubtful that you can find out all you need to know without seeing your party in person—unless, of course, you plan to use him just to fill in some gaps in your information.

It's worth noting that the telephone can prove next to worthless if you are doing an important investigative story. In 1969, in one of the most important journalistic scoops of recent years, *Life* revealed that former U.S. Supreme Court Justice Abe Fortas had accepted $20,000 from a family foundation headed by Louis E. Wolfson, a convicted stock manipulator, apparently in return for advising the foundation on how to make charitable contributions. Although Fortas later returned the money, the disclosure that he had accepted it in the first place ultimately led to his resignation.

The reporter who tracked down the story was William Lambert. He had previously won a Pulitzer Prize while employed by the Portland *Oregonian*. And he makes this telling comment about the Fortas story and about using the telephone on any kind of investigative article:

"I've never worked on a story where I found such extreme reluctance to talk. When you take on a Supreme Court Justice, everyone dives underneath his desk. One guy said, 'Don't ask me any questions. Don't even tell me anything. I just don't want to know.'

"The telephone has ruined many good investigative reporters. And it certainly won't work in a situation like the Fortas story. You have to get out and eyeball your sources, because ultimately it's their confidence in your integrity that will get you the story."

3. How many other people do you plan to interview? If you plan to interview just one man about a subject to which you plan to devote a half dozen or more typewritten pages, be wary of interviewing him over the telephone—unless you are already in possession of considerable background information. You, he, or both of you may overlook matters of vital concern.

If you plan to conduct brief interviews with several men, you are on safer ground in using the telephone. You are less apt to fall on your face if one interview doesn't work out. You are more apt to learn all the important things you should learn. And you are more likely to produce a well-rounded article. In fact, it is safe to say that the telephone is often most useful to journalists when they need to produce a relatively short roundup article that includes information from several organizations or several people.

4. Finally, how complex is the information you wish to obtain? If you will be talking about highly technical matters of which you have little or no understanding, be hesitant to resort to the telephone. A telephone conversation is rarely the place to ask basic, orientation-type questions. If you do ask such questions and if you don't quickly grasp what you are told, you run the risk that both you and the organization you represent will look poorly in the interviewee's eyes. You also increase your chances of making an error.

So, before turning to the telephone, always be sure that you know the fundamental concepts and terminology in use in the field you are inquiring about. If you are talking with a man in person, the situation will be different. It may be possible for him to refer to pictures, charts, and other visual aids to make his explanations clearer.

To sum up what's been said so far: The telephone is a highly useful journalistic tool. But it involves a higher degree of risk than face-to-face interviewing. So it's best used for relatively short interviews on subjects in which the interviewer already has considerable grounding.

When you do use the telephone, here are a few tips designed to help you get the most out of it:

Get to the point right away. In a telephone interview it is best to avoid opening pleasantries altogether, unless you're a personal friend of the person you're calling. State who you are, what you're connected with, and why you're calling. Then ask if the interviewee has a few minutes to answer your questions. If you have no more than four or five questions to ask, make that plain. It will tend to reassure the interviewee that he won't be on the telephone for the rest of the afternoon.

Be flexible. If the man indicates that he's tied up and would like you to call back at a later hour or day, go along with him if at all possible. There's absolutely no advantage to trying to force a person to talk with you at a time that is inconvenient to him. He may decide that he doesn't want to talk at all.

Plot your questions in advance and make them as specific as possible. In an earlier chapter I indicated that I always do this in advance of all kinds of interviews but that many other journalists go into interviews with only a few key questions in mind and still produce successful results. In a telephone interview, however, I don't think there's much room for argument. You must know precisely what you want to find out.

Consider tape recording the interview. Although I'm no advocate of tape recorders in interviewing, I think a much stronger case can be made for using them in extended telephone interviews than in face-to-face interviews. The conversation seems to go much faster in the one than the other. And scribbling, which is often very close to real scribbling, is much more difficult.

A tape recorder can ease both these problems. And if the

interview is not too long, having the tape transcribed should not be a problem.

Earlier it was indicated that it is usually wise to ask a man if you can tape record a face-to-face interview. Whether this is also the wise thing to do in the case of a telephone interview is questionable. If you do tell the interviewee and if he does not know you, the knowledge that you are taping the interview may make him more cautious than ever. Also, he may insist on seeing the results of the interview prior to publication, even though you may be rushing to get it into print.

On the other hand, if you don't tell him, there is a question of whether you are being fair. Some people would consider the taping an invasion of privacy.

The way to resolve the problem is to consider in advance whether you are likely to be talking about embarrassing or potentially embarrassing subjects. If not, then you may do well to err on the side of caution and *not* tell him you are recording the interview. This is especially acceptable, I think, if the interviewee will have a chance to see how you plan to use the material he gives you before you publish it. If you will be talking about subjects on which most men would employ more than normal discretion, however, it is a different matter. Then you will have to consider the circumstances and weigh whether you would be unfair in not disclosing that the interview is being recorded.

Another way to look at this problem is to remember that, from the legal standpoint, the real question is not whether you tape record a telephone interview but what you do with the information you obtain. If subsequent publication or other use of the information would leave you or the organization that employs you open to charges of libel or invasion of privacy, you had better be cautious about what you say or write.

Finally, if you take notes instead of using a tape recorder, go over them immediately after the interview. When I conduct a face-to-face interview I sometimes go over my notes right away, sometimes a few hours later, sometimes the next day. After a telephone interview, however, I flesh them out at once, without exception. That is largely because the notes are likely to be sketchier than those I take in a standard interview.

Other journalists of my acquaintance seem to find the same thing. Also, the details of the conversation seem to fade more quickly from one's mind. It is important to combat these drawbacks to the telephone interview at once.

When I refer to a group interview I mean the kind of interview in which one or two journalists interview a number of men or women at the same time. I do not refer to that rare aberration in journalism in which a number of representatives of the same publication interview just one man at the same time. The latter kind of interview is usually—although not always—a patent waste of time and manpower.

One of the worst examples I have heard of took place within very recent years at the offices of one of the nation's major newsweekly magazines. No fewer than 12 editors sat down with a man who was an expert in a certain area of finance. Each editor was allowed—and expected—to ask just one question. The result was a relatively brief and successful question-and-answer story that could easily have been handled by just one or two editors.

As this anecdote suggests, the results of a group interview that is held by a magazine or newspaper are often presented in question-and-answer form. When well done, this kind of interview can be highly successful because it is apt to be highly readable. If it is handled poorly, however, the resulting story can be very confusing. I have even known instances in which no story resulted at all.

An occasional proponent of the group interview is *Playboy*. Perhaps once or twice a year it assembles a number of experts on some such topic as religion or criminality and asks them to expound their views. The result is presented in question-and-answer form, with, of course, *Playboy* doing the questioning.

And, very frankly, I think the result is often unsuccessful—in sharp contrast, incidentally, to the magazine's one-man interviews. I believe the group interviews are often unsuccessful for a very simple reason. The magazine includes too many interviewees—sometimes as many as eight or nine.

This makes it hard for the reader to keep them all straight. If he is interested in what a given man says, he must often look back to the introduction to remind himself who the man is and what his credentials are. To make a reader keep checking back so as to know what is going on is simply not good journalism.

This and other experiences with the group interview suggest one simple rule for conducting it, presuming you are planning to publish the results in question-and-answer form. Never include more than six men in the group. Five, in fact, is a perfectly acceptable number, and so is four. Three, of course, would seem to be the minimum number to include if it's a group that you are thinking of.

Radio and television, you may have noticed, rarely violate this precept. Almost always they interview no more than three or four men at a time. And yet television at least benefits from the fact that its audience can see the interviewees and more easily remember who is who than it is possible to do when an interview is reported in printed matter.

The problems connected with interviewing several men at once are severe enough so that I would like to suggest an alternative that I have occasionally found quite successful. It is sometimes possible to interview a group of men separately, ask them all the same questions, yet still report their answers in question-and-answer form or something very similar. This approach may work especially well if the interviewer has a chance to check the result with the various interviewees prior to publication.

Nonetheless, this approach can usually work only when your primary goal is to seek information and advice that can be passed along to your readers. If you wish to present a discussion-type interview, in which there may be subtle conflicts of opinion and in which no definite conclusions may be reached, it is almost imperative that you bring the interviewees together. They must be given a chance to thrash out their differences face to face if the interview is to be really successful.

The other rules for conducting a group interview are not really much different from those for conducting a one-man interview. But a few points do deserve special emphasis.

It is probably better to enter such an interview with many fewer questions than you might bring to a one-man interview. A group interview has a tendency to create its own momentum and to get into conversational facets that you may never have thought of. Thus, if you have too many predetermined questions, you may never get to them all.

It is doubly important that the journalist in charge of the interview maintain strict control of it. This is much harder to do than is the case in one-man interviews. The journalist must not only make sure that the discussion never gets too far off track, but, even more important, he must make sure that all the participants have a chance to speak their piece. It is easy enough for one or two eloquent—or voluble—men to dominate an interview if the interviewer does not take care. This can cause hurt feelings and also result in loss of valuable commentary.

Finally, unless the group interview is a brainstorming session whose results will be used primarily as background information by the journalists present, it will probably be most unwise to try to cover it with paper and pencil. It may, of course, be possible to have a stenographer present whose sole duty will be to take down what is said rather than to ask questions or otherwise participate in the discussion. If you can't or don't want to use a stenographer, then you will almost certainly be wise to employ a tape recorder, although the problem of transcribing the results—and of knowing who said what—will be a big one for the typist involved.

The group interview is not common in written journalism. Perhaps that is because of the inherent problems it creates. Nonetheless, when well handled it can be very successful indeed. Certainly, the television networks have proved this time and again, although it is obvious that they operate under much easier conditions in conducting this type of interview than any magazine or newspaper does.

A few years ago a reporter for the *New York Times* appeared in the office of an upper-middle-echelon official of the U.S. State Department and asked to interview him about a certain diplomatic problem of the day. The State Department official said he'd be glad to answer any questions the reporter might pose, provided it was clearly understood that the entire interview would be off the record.

Whereupon the reporter stood up, closed his notebook, and said he could obtain the information he needed elsewhere— and obtain it on the record. And he did. As a matter of fact, he obtained it from a State Department official of higher status.

This incident is not unique. Plenty of reporters refuse to hold off-the-record interviews. And there is a great deal of logic in their refusal. After all, it is a journalist's chief function to produce intelligent, interesting copy. But if he can't report what he has been told, why listen to the telling in the first place —especially if he believes he can obtain the same story from another source?

But before dismissing the off-the-record interview as a waste of time—which it, nonetheless, often is—a few comments are in order.

First, if you are ever faced with the seeming necessity of conducting an off-the-record interview, be sure that you and the man you are interviewing understand what the term really means. To most journalists the term means just what it seems to mean: None of the material obtained in the interview may be reported in any fashion whatsoever. The typical layman, however, is not apt to be versed in the ins and outs of journalism. In insisting that an interview be off the record, he may only be saying, "Use the material I am giving you if you wish, but make sure that nobody knows it came from me." In other words, he may be doing no more than trying to hold a background interview, the results of which can be reported without attribution to the source. It is also possible that, although he may seem to want to put the entire interview off the record, he may really be seeking to protect only a few individual statements.

The fact is that even experienced, sophisticated laymen aren't always knowledgeable about the niceties of journalism. Thus, shortly after the Eisenhower Administration first came to power, Secretary of the Treasury George Humphrey held a luncheon for some of Washington's financial reporters. The new Secretary talked rather freely about some of the trouble he was having in persuading the Pentagon to hold down its requests for more money.

Without having so specified, he assumed that the entire luncheon was off the record. But the reporters assumed no such thing. They believed that it was a "background lunch" and that they could report what they had learned, provided they did not attribute it to Humphrey.

And in fact a number of them did report it. One of them was a personal friend of mine. Humphrey just happened to see his story in print first, called him in, and gave him a strong tongue-lashing. It was not the first time that a man new to the power corridors of Washington had not understood the ground rules of journalism.

Second, before rejecting or condemning off-the-record interviews out of hand, remember that different journalists work in different environments. Some operate in situations in which off-the-record interviews are held much more often than elsewhere.

This is certainly the case with the Washington press corps. Its members sometimes hold such interviews—occasionally unexpectedly—at lunches, dinner parties, and in other less social circumstances. Why do they agree to this?

One answer is that they sometimes have to. The officials with whom they talk may function at such a high level of government that they can dictate their own terms. And in some instances these officials may prefer the off-the-record interview to a background interview.

Another answer is that they may not wish to alienate a useful source of information. The official who insists on talking off the record today may be quite willing to talk on the record a month or two hence. But if he has been rebuffed in the first instance he may turn to another journalist than the one who turned him down.

Then too, it is occasionally possible to report an off-the-record interview at some later date. This opportunity presented itself not so long ago to C. L. Sulzberger, the noted foreign affairs correspondent for the *New York Times*.

In 1969, Sulzberger interviewed Charles de Gaulle, who had resigned as President of France only two months earlier. The two talked on many subjects—French-American relations, the North Atlantic Treaty Organization, the Vietnam War, and other problems of the world. But even though Sulzberger had previously interviewed de Gaulle, the French leader stipulated that this particular interview was to be off the record.

He did, however, permit Sulzberger to take extensive notes. And when the French leader died late in 1970, Sulzberger no longer felt bound by his pledge. The result was a front-page story in the *Times*.

Still another answer is that, even though a reporter may not be able to publish the results of an off-the-record interview, he may obtain invaluable confidential judgments or facts. He may then be able to use these judgments or facts to appraise the accuracy or meaning of the words or deeds of other people.

Politicians who weigh what they say, officials who fear retaliation from their superiors, ordinary citizens who worry about persecution or prosecution would often refuse to talk to reporters if they thought their words would be reported. Yet if it were not possible to talk to such persons on an off-the-record basis, much priceless information would never come to light or, if it did, would have to be laboriously gathered by other means. Moreover, much that is gathered would not be subject to the intensive cross-examination that can sometimes be obtained in an off-the-record interview.

Finally, nothing precludes a reporter from following up on an off-the-record interview. In other words, even though he hasn't obtained a useful story from such an interview, he may have obtained a useful lead. He may be able to go to other sources, verify what he has learned in the off-the-record interview, and write a story that in no way involves the man with whom he first talked.

It was, in fact, just such a tip that led to William Lambert's exposé of Justice Abe Fortas. Lambert was in Washington some months before he broke the Fortas story, talking confidentially with various government officials about a number of matters. One of them, who was on a fairly low level, just happened to remark, "Why don't you look into the relationship between Abe Fortas and Louis Wolfson?" That simple hint was enough to set Lambert off and running.

The off-the-record interview is not confined to Washington. Crime reporters, for example, sometimes hold off-the-record interviews with police officers. In some such cases the information the reporters obtain is off the record only temporarily.

Thus the police may know certain facts about a murder or some other crime that they have not yet solved. For one reason or another they may not want these facts revealed to the public before the crime is solved. But they may tell trusted reporters what they know—with the clear-cut understanding that the information cannot be reported until a later date.

This brings up the one rule that can be flatly and unequivocally stated in regard to off-the-record interviews. Once you have agreed to interview someone on this basis, keep your word. You will probably never get another interview from the person if you don't.

Otherwise, no rules can be given for this kind of interview—only questions that must be asked. The individual journalist will have to answer them in light of the circumstances in which he finds himself.

Does off the record really mean off the record?

Could you obtain the information you seek from somebody else?

Is the person you are interviewing someone with whom you are likely to have a continuing relationship and from whom you might obtain on-the-record stories in the future?

Does the interviewee have seemingly valid reasons for wanting to talk off the record?

Do you operate in an environment in which the off-the-record interview is, if not commonplace, more frequent than in other areas of journalism?

Finally, what kind of story are you writing? "If you're writing a newspaper story," says Richard Hammer, editor of the *New York Times* The Week in Review, "it may be perfectly all right to talk with people on an off-the-record basis. You are writing for the immediate moment. You may need to use a particular source again. And if you report material that was told to you on an off-the-record basis, there's a good chance that the source will be discovered or at least guessed at.

"But if you're writing a book," Hammer adds, "be most reluctant to talk on an off-the-record basis. While I was preparing my own book, *The Court-Martial of Lt. Calley,* a number of people said they would tell me things on an off-the-record basis. I told them nothing doing, and in almost every case got them to come around to my way of thinking.

"When you're writing a book, you are not writing for the immediate moment. You are writing something that is supposed to last and that people can go back to. If you accept a lot of material on an off-the-record basis, the book will have little real value. It will fade into nothing. Besides, a book is published six, eight, 10 months after you finish it. So there's less chance that the material you use will harm people from whom you obtained it, more chance that some of it will have crept into the public domain anyway."

You will have to be fair and discreet in answering these questions, but there's no need to be ridiculous. Some men have tried to put entire press conferences off the record, even though as many as 250 people have been present. The experienced journalist scoffs at such naïveté. And well he should. What is off the record when only one or two men hear it is hardly off the record when 250 people do so.

8. The Right of Review

Late in 1966 Jacqueline Onassis—then still Jacqueline Kennedy—brought suit against Harper & Row, the book publishers, and *Look,* the former biweekly magazine. The suit was designed to prevent the publishers from bringing out a book about the assassination of her husband and the magazine from printing a serialization of the same. The book was entitled *The Death of a President.*

The suit, and all the events surrounding it, produced front-page newspaper headlines and a spate of magazine cover stories all over the world. One famous American magazine said it involved "the book of the decade" and "the crime of the century."

Whatever the merits of the suit, the facts are fairly plain. The Kennedy family, and Jacqueline Kennedy in particular, had agreed to help William Manchester, a onetime reporter for the Baltimore *Sun* who had already authored one book about President Kennedy, to write another, dealing with his assassination in Dallas, Texas, on November 22, 1963. If Manchester was not what is known as an official biographer, he came about as close to it as it is possible to come. Among other things, the Kennedys agreed to grant him interviews and access to written materials that they denied to other authors, some of whom had

114

equal or bigger reputations. Mrs. Kennedy, in fact, told another would-be chronicler that she had "hired" Manchester to write the book in order "to protect President Kennedy and the truth."

For his part, Manchester agreed to let the Kennedys review his book prior to publication. This permission to review, in fact, was included in an 11-point contract that he and the Kennedys both signed.

Although the precise meaning of this right of review was not spelled out in most of the magazine and newspaper stories about the suit, the implication was clear. In the Kennedys' opinion, and apparently in the opinion of many other people who were also involved, it meant that the late President's family had the right to change or to delete any passages that they wished to. And exercise that right, if that's what it was, they definitely decided to do.

Several old friends of the family, including some who had been politically close to the President, first read the book and suggested some changes. Apparently these changes were primarily designed to rid the book of certain seeming prejudices against President Lyndon B. Johnson, Kennedy's successor. And apparently Manchester agreed to make most of the changes.

Then the book's magazine serial rights were sold to *Look* and complications began to develop. The Kennedy family was concerned that the serialization might distort certain passages in the book. Yet in selling the right to serialize the book Manchester had granted *Look* editorial control of his material.

In the meantime Mrs. Kennedy herself had read at least certain portions of the book. Four months after the late President's assassination, she had let Manchester interview her for periods totaling 10 hours. The interviews had been tape recorded. And now, upon reading the book, she felt that he had reported her emotions and inward feelings too faithfully, and she became determined to blue-pencil certain passages she did not like. Nat-

urally she ran into some resistance from Manchester, Harper &
Row, and *Look*.

Whereupon she obtained a temporary court injunction block-
ing publication of both the book and the serialization. Her
basic charge was that Manchester had broken their contract.

Ultimately the case was settled out of court. Both book and
magazine serialization reached print—but only after certain
other changes and deletions had been made. Thus it was reported that *Look* had agreed to delete some 1,600 words of its
60,000-word serialization and to soften or otherwise change
certain other passages to which Mrs. Kennedy objected.

Judging from all the reports of the case, many misunder-
standings developed on all sides. But whatever else may be
true, this much seems sure: William Manchester made a mistake in the very beginning by agreeing to let the Kennedys review his book, especially since that permission apparently carried with it the right to command changes and deletions. As
Theodore H. White, author of *The Making of the President,* an
even more famous book about President Kennedy, put it, "A
man who writes on public affairs should refuse to commit to
anybody the right to review his copy."

This whole story brings up a problem that often confronts
magazines and, to a lesser extent, other journalistic media in
more subtle and ambiguous form. The problem is simply this:
Should journalists voluntarily check their stories with the sources
from whom they obtained their information, in order to assure
the stories' factual and, possibly, interpretive accuracy? In thus
stating the question I am assuming that when they do thus
check their stories journalistic media do not grant, and do not
intend to grant, any contractual right of review such as was
enjoyed by the Kennedys. Rather, they are merely seeking factual corrections and any other suggestions the sources may want
to make. They are not relinquishing their right to reject the

suggestions and possibly even the factual corrections if they so wish.

This is an important point. It is important partly because it is the way in which all or nearly all magazines that presently follow this policy do operate and partly because it is the only sensible way in which to operate.

Newspapermen rarely have to face this issue. They almost never submit copy to the sources of their stories prior to publication. A major reason is that, unless they are writing the kind of feature story that can be held up for a few days, they don't have time. Today's news must be printed tomorrow.

To be sure, newspapermen will sometimes telephone the source of an article to double-check the accuracy of certain facts and figures that they have been given. But this is a far cry from checking out a whole story.

In many ways it is well that newspapers do not often face this problem. More than magazines, more than radio and television, they are the chief defenders of this country's freedom of the press and of the public's right to know. Even when a contract granting the right to review does not exist, submitting copy to the source of a story runs the inherent risk that the source may attempt to censor the copy. And no believer in freedom of the press wants that. It is better that misstatements of fact sometimes creep into newspaper pages—and many more do than are ever acknowledged—than that the newspapers submit to outside checking.

Why, then, do many magazines follow the policy of checking out their stories before going into print? The magazines would reply that they seek total factual accuracy. And, ironically, many old-line newspapermen would scoff at them. They would argue that any editor or writer who can't get the facts straight in the first place doesn't belong in the field of journalism.

Like many other arguments based on pride or contempt, this

one is only partially true. Although it may be more than half true, it is surely not the whole truth.

Obviously, it is incumbent upon any journalist worthy of the name to get his facts straight. And most of them do, most of the time—probably almost all of the time. They wouldn't last long in their profession if they didn't.

But it is hard to imagine that there is any journalist alive who has not made some misstatement of fact in some story, somewhere, sometime. Whether the misstatement was trivial does not matter. It has been there.

Sometimes the fault for errors of fact rests with the journalist himself. He may have misread or misheard. Or he may have failed to check information that he should have checked.

But to say that the fault may sometimes be the journalist's is not to say that this is always the case. A source the journalist relied on and had good reason to rely on may have given him erroneous information. Not deliberately, but through a failure of his memory. Dates, figures, and other kinds of precise data often fade from people's memories or are remembered erroneously.

Speaking in a somewhat different context, Sir Winston Churchill once put the problem very neatly by saying, "During my life, I have often had to eat my own words, and on the whole I have found them a wholesome diet." Although journalists do not have to eat their own words very often, just about all of them have had to munch on one or two.

So there is solid reason for checking out copy with its sources prior to publication if you are in a position to do so. Factual and other kinds of errors do creep in. Anyone who has ever edited other people's articles or sent them out for checking can attest to this.

In fact, many leading magazines insist on this policy. *Reader's Digest* is a notable case in point.

Many well-known individual authors do the same thing. Stewart Alsop, the onetime newspaper columnist who subsequently wrote for the *Saturday Evening Post* and who now writes for *Newsweek,* is certainly one of the most distinguished, respected journalists in the country. Yet in his book *The Center: People and Power in Political Washington,* he unabashedly concedes in two different instances that he has submitted whole articles to outside sources for factual checking.

Thus, in 1962, he collaborated with another journalist to write an article for the *Saturday Evening Post* about the Cuban missile crisis. The article dealt in particular with all the debates that went on within the Kennedy Administration on how to handle the crisis and with the final decision on how to prevent the Soviet Union from planting further missiles in Cuba.

To write the article Alsop and his co-author had to draw on many sources, some secret or semisecret. To make sure that they had reported the whole story correctly, they submitted it to President Kennedy himself. Thus, Alsop writes, "Kennedy read the piece for accuracy and proposed a couple of minor changes."

The other instance involved a chapter in *The Center* itself. The chapter dealt with the nature and state of the Defense Department. To write it, Alsop interviewed the then Secretary of Defense, Robert S. McNamara. Among other things, Alsop and McNamara discussed nuclear war, and Alsop wrote that McNamara had said, "It's extremely important to realize that a full nuclear exchange could destroy both sides."

Subsequently Alsop asked McNamara to check the chapter for accuracy. In *The Center* Alsop writes, "The paragraph above came back unchanged, except that the 'c' in the word 'could' in the last sentence was crossed out and a 'w' neatly substituted."

A small change, a tiny change, but an all-important change. Important not only to the accuracy of Alsop's book but also because of the indication it provides to the whole thinking of

Robert McNamara, widely regarded as the most influential member of the Cabinets of both President Kennedy and President Johnson.

Nor are these isolated examples of stories that have been checked with their sources. Early in 1970, the *New York Times'* C. L. Sulzberger interviewed Georges Pompidou, President of France. Although Pompidou did not ask to see Sulzberger's article before it went to press, he did insist on seeing the transcript of the interview itself. He not only reviewed it, but he also amended it. Sulzberger had to grant him this privilege in order to obtain the interview in the first place.

Ensuring factual accuracy is the overriding reason for submitting articles to sources. But sometimes there are additional benefits to be derived from this process. For example, upon seeing an article a source may suggest the inclusion of additional information that did not come up during the course of the interview on which the article is based. Occasionally such additions may add real value to the story in question. Or a source may suggest a minor deletion or change in wording that will save some person unnecessary embarrassment, yet not cause any damage to the story.

Personally, I believe that the case for checking out articles is much stronger than the case against it—all other things, including the nature of the publication one works for, being equal. But plenty of publications do not check out their articles, often as a matter of principle. And there's no question that there are risks involved in doing so.

One of them is loss of time. If only one or two sources must review an article, it can often be checked out in two or three days. But this rule is not invariable, and occasionally the process may take a couple of weeks.

An even more frustrating situation may arise if an article has been prepared for an interviewee's byline and, upon seeing it, he demands a lot of unreasonable changes. Then negotiations may drag on for a month or more. Meanwhile, of course, the article will remain unpublished.

The chief risk to checking stories with their sources has already been indicated. Pressure, occasionally amounting to something akin to attempted censorship, can and sometimes is brought to bear to change wordings, delete passages, or even kill articles outright. I don't believe that such extreme pressure is common, but it does occur.

A recent and somewhat unusual case involved the widely publicized television documentary *The Selling of the Pentagon*. Early in 1971, the Columbia Broadcasting System aired the hour-long documentary in some 200 cities across the country. The film's message was plain: The nation's Defense Department was spending millions of dollars each year trying to persuade the people of this country of the rightness of its various points of view. In the process, it was sometimes deliberately deceiving them and the various journalistic media as well.

The documentary created an instant furor. Several members of Congress angrily denounced it. A few believed that, in preparing the documentary, CBS itself had been guilty of deceit. Indeed, one subcommittee of the House of Representatives served a subpoena on the network, demanding that it turn over all the film, sound recordings, transcripts, and other materials that had gone into the making of the documentary, whether those materials had actually been used or not.

But CBS regarded the issue as one of freedom of the press from legislative surveillance. It objected in particular to handing over those materials that had been gathered but not actually used. It said these were no different from a newspaper reporter's notebooks.

When the network refused to comply fully with the subpoena, the House subcommittee unanimously voted to cite its president for contempt of Congress. Ultimately, the House of Representatives as a whole refused to uphold this citation, and the issue was dropped. Meanwhile, the documentary had won a Peabody Prize.

All this pressure from certain members of Congress was, of course, after the fact. It was not designed to change a documentary that had already been televised but to make the television networks think twice before airing a similar show in the future, lest they perhaps lose their government-issued licenses to operate. Nonetheless, the pressure just shows how far some people are willing to go in trying to thwart the public's right to know.

The debate over the *The Selling of the Pentagon* had not been fully resolved before a similar but even more important case thrust itself upon the conscience of the country. The *New York Times,* the Washington *Post,* and a few other well-known newspapers began publishing extensive excerpts from the so-called Pentagon Papers, a secret, massive, government-ordered history of the major decisions involved in the United States' participation in the Vietnam War.

The history was not entirely complimentary to certain former officials of the U.S. Government. The newspapers had obtained it by clandestine means. And hardly had they begun its publication, in serial form, before the Nixon Administration obtained a temporary court injunction forbidding its further use. The Administration charged that publication would cause irreparable damage to the nation's security.

This was as heavy-handed an attempt as there could be to prevent publication of an article or, more exactly, a series of articles. From a legal standpoint, the basic issue was between the Constitutionally guaranteed rights of freedom of speech and of the press and the government's right to protect the country against unwarranted disclosures harmful to its safety. The *Times* conceded that further publication might embarrass certain individuals and the Government as a whole. It also conceded that one could conceive of situations in which publication of secret material would cause serious damage to the nation.

But it refused to admit that such damage would be caused by publication of the rest of the Pentagon Papers.

Successive courts, including the U.S. Supreme Court, agreed with the newspapers. As Judge Murray I. Gurfein, one of the lower court justices, put it, "A cantankerous press, an obstinate press, a ubiquitous press must be suffered by those in authority in order to preserve the even greater values of freedom of expression and the right of the people to know."

The upshot was, of course, that the remainder of the excerpts from the Pentagon Papers were published. To date, the nation does not seem to have suffered much, if at all, from the result.

The typical journalist will not have to deal with censorship attempts of such far-reaching consequence. But he may have to deal with cases in which the basic issues will be just as significant, even if the results are not as important. He may also have to deal with people or organizations that are just as hard to handle.

I know of one instance in which a company president decided that he did not wish to release any of the contents of an interview he had already given. The issue in which the interview was to appear was already on the presses, however, and the editor told him nothing could be done. Happily, the editor was the kind of man who would have told him nothing could be done anyway.

Pressure—and I mean pressure, as opposed to politely worded requests—can also take the form of threats to withdraw or withhold advertising. Again, this kind of pressure is not common. But it does occur. And it can be tougher to withstand, because the threat may be transmitted to a publication's sales (advertising) department rather than to its editors. By and large, sales managers are not well known for standing up for editorial integrity when advertising is threatened. It is no accident that Harold Ross, *The New Yorker*'s most famous editor, strictly forbade any advertising space salesmen to even set foot on the floor where the magazine's editors were located. He enforced the ban, too.

There are no easy rules for resisting this kind of pressure. Much depends on the particular circumstances, on the attitude of the sales manager involved, and, more importantly, on that of the publisher. Some publishers have strong scruples about not interfering with the work of editors they trust. Other publishers have even stronger scruples about not interfering with advertising revenue.

Just a few years ago, the *Wall Street Journal* reported that a survey of 162 newspaper business and financial editors had indicated that almost 23 percent of them were routinely required to puff up, alter, or downgrade business stories at the request of advertisers. The requests for such changes were usually transmitted through the newspapers' own advertising departments. And even when the editors fought against them, they often found that they could not obtain the support of their own publishers.

The most common kind of pressure to force changes in editorial copy comes through force of personality. Instead of returning an article by mail with whatever factual corrections and suggestions he may have, a story source calls an editor up and, in effect, tries to browbeat him into making certain changes that are neither necessary nor called for.

Some editors and reporters can stand up very well under this kind of pressure. Others tend to buckle. Two or three of the latter kind have asked me on occasion how to handle veritable demands for changes in their copy. And I have always recommended the same course: Tell your source that you will jot down his requests, then pass them on to the editor in chief. After all, one of the top editor's jobs is to handle the hot ones.

A good editor or reporter does not pass on many things like this, however. Normally he should be able to handle requests for changes himself. It's his job, too, to protect the independence and integrity of his own publication.

I still vividly remember what I hope is the only instance in which I submitted to pressure for unnecessary changes in editorial copy. The article discussed so-called venture capital firms. In essence, these firms provide start-up or additional capital to new, little businesses that seem to have good ideas and good executives but not enough capital with which to get going. Often the little businesses are operating on the technological frontiers of American industry.

Partly for this reason, venture capital firms constitute an important factor in the American economy. But they are not well known because they guard their operations with a great deal of secrecy. At that time at least, there were only about 10 or a dozen of real consequence, and I had been fortunate to get in to see three of them.

Upon seeing the article I had written, the president of one firm called up and said it looked fine. Five minutes later the vice-president of one of the other firms called to request four or five minor changes involving perhaps a total of a dozen words. The changes seemed justified, and I agreed to make them.

Although I thought the conversation was over, it wasn't. For the next 40 minutes the vice-president talked on, indicating a vague, general dissatisfaction with the article. I was puzzled. I tried several times to find out what was bothering him but couldn't seem to pin him down. He didn't seem to have any other specific changes to request.

Finally, however, the nature of his anxiety became somewhat clearer. He told me that the article would have to be cleared by his firm's tax lawyers before he could agree to the release of the information pertaining to his firm. (To the best of my knowledge, his firm was doing nothing wrong, but I later learned from another person that the vice-president feared that the article would somehow lead to an investigation by the Internal Revenue Service.)

It was late on a very hot Friday afternoon in late May. By the time the vice-president finally came to the point I was tired and out of sorts. Reluctantly I agreed to his request. And no sooner had I left the office than I knew I had done the wrong thing.

On Monday morning I returned to the office. I didn't bother to take the matter up with the editor. Instead, I immediately wrote a letter to the vice-president. I made it as courteous as I could and told him that we would stand by the few minor changes I had agreed to make. In fact, I added, we would be glad to consider any others he might want to suggest provided there were sound editorial reasons for considering them. But under no circumstances, I emphasized, could we let his tax lawyers review the article, especially if that were to mean that they had veto power over it or any of its parts. To do so, I pointed out, would be to surrender the editorial independence of our own magazine.

I never heard from the vice-president again. And I do not imagine that he heard from the Internal Revenue Service either. In any case, the article was published, and his firm is still in business.

Although actual pressure to change articles is not common, requests for changes are. Sometimes the requests are fully justified. Sometimes they are not justified at all.

Some people make their requests deferentially. Some make them matter-of-factly. Some make them abruptly. Some request the change or deletion of only one or two words in a 25-page article. Others request sweeping changes in whole paragraphs or even in whole pages.

The worst offenders are those rare people who make only a few changes in a long article, yet insist on retyping the whole article before returning it. It is then necessary for the editor to compare the retyped article with the original one, line for line, in order to determine what the requests are.

How can an editor determine whether it is right to make requested changes or not? There can be no easy, quick answer to this question. So much depends on the nature of an individual article. But asking yourself these few questions may help you come to a decision:

How many requests are there? It is safe to say, as a rough rule of thumb, that the more requests for changes a person makes the more cause you have to suspect that he has engaged in what some editors call doodling. That is, he has sought change for the sake of change. This presumes, of course, that the changes do not involve corrections of factual errors.

Of course, there are always exceptions to this general rule. I know of one case in which a corporate official requested 20 changes in a 20-page article. Although all the changes were minor, only three or four of them involved factual matters. The magazine in question made all of them, however, because all of them seemed justified.

This brings up a second key question: How valid are the reasons for the requests?

Some years ago I had occasion to interview Charles Brower, then chairman of Batten, Barton, Durstine & Osborn, the advertising agency, and several other company chairmen on how they had gone about picking their successors as presidents. Brower is a very droll man, and the interview he gave me was frequently punctuated by my own laughter and that of his public relations director.

Among other things, I asked him how important a man's wife was if he was under consideration for a company presidency. His quick retort was that a wife should be given no consideration at all, so long as she was "white and presentable."

If anyone else had been in the room, he would have known

without any question that there was not the slightest trace of racial prejudice in Brower's remark. As a matter of fact, I included it in the article I wrote without even thinking about that possibility.

Back came the article, however, with the request that this statement be deleted. Upon seeing it in typewritten form, Brower believed that it could be interpreted as evidence of racial prejudice. And what would have made it all the worse from his standpoint, his public relations director told me, is that he had been active in the civil rights movement and had gone out of his way to recruit black employees for his own firm.

I didn't like making the deletion, because businessmen don't often make colorful or even semicolorful remarks. But I made it. There is no point in embarrassing a man unnecessarily. Besides, the remark was not necessary to an understanding of the point Brower had been trying to make.

Many requests for changes, other than changes in fact, involve matters like this. That's why it is often wise to find out the reason for the request.

Do the suggested changes improve the article? There is little point in acceding to them unless they do, presuming, of course, that they are not made with the thought of saving someone from unnecessary embarrassment.

How is the request made? The occasional person who abruptly demands changes as though this were his God-given right is given short shrift by most editors I have known, other things being equal. And well he should be. The chance to see an article before it goes into print is not a right, but a privilege.

Finally, what is the background of the person making the request? The more experience a man has had with the press, the less consideration he should be given. For example, men who enter politics have sometimes made statements to journalists that have had unfortunate national repercussions and that, in retrospect, they probably wished they had never made. In short, they have committed bloopers.

In most such cases I doubt that they had a chance to review what they said before it went into print because they were dealing with newspapermen. It may seem unfair that a man who goes into politics does not usually have a chance to change or retract unfortunate remarks before publication. But that is one of the prices one pays for going into politics, although I think it is only fair to add that much too much is sometimes made of the verbal indiscretions politicians occasionally commit.

Thus, in 1970, during the trial of Charles Manson for the so-called Sharon Tate murders, President Nixon publicly announced that Manson was "guilty, directly or indirectly, of eight murders without reason." Obviously, Nixon had prejudged the case and violated the nation's long-standing assumption that a man is innocent until proved guilty.

The President's unexpected off-the-cuff pronouncement produced banner headlines all across the country, plus the temporary threat of a mistrial. Naturally, he soon retracted the statement altogether. But the damage had been done. In addition to widespread news stories, all kinds of commentary poured forth from newspaper columnists and editorial writers.

Two columnists for the *New York Times* took what seems to me the right tack. One said, "Mr. Nixon merely talked before thinking and is entitled to a presumption of innocence, which he later granted to Mr. Manson." The other added, "What this incident seems to say about Mr. Nixon is that, like most mortals, he is capable of indiscretions, even large ones, in moments of heat."

Nonetheless, considering the nature of our political process, it is probably just as well that politicians are held accountable for the off-the-cuff remarks they make in public. Surely one criterion by which to judge a politician—although not necessarily the most important one—is how well he handles questions from the press. The man who frequently blows his cool, as the saying goes, or who commonly speaks before thinking may commit serious indiscretions in dealing with foreign nations. In this connection I have heard it said that one reason President John F. Kennedy was so successful with journalists was that he rarely answered a question without first thinking how his answer would look in a headline.

But most people don't go into politics. And most don't deal frequently with journalists. And if a man has in good faith given a good interview—in which he has made one blooper that he would like to change—I believe that he deserves consideration.

That does not mean that his request should be automatically granted. Much depends on what he said, why he said it—and in connection with what article. But it does mean that his request should be looked upon with more sympathy than that of someone who often deals with the press and who knows, or should know, the risk he takes in making rash, ill-considered remarks.

These are the questions one can quickly ask himself before acceding to any requests for changes other than changes in fact. Yet the best way to deal with the problem of requested changes is through preventive action. The reporter or editor who sends out an article for checking should make plain that in so doing he is not giving the source of his story editorial control over it. One way to do this is to ask for "corrections of any factual errors there may be and other *suggestions* you may have." Some people won't take the hint. They'll still act as if they had a right to change the article as they see fit. But most people will take it.

Early in this chapter it was indicated that newspapers do not often let outside sources review their articles prior to publication. Yet they sometimes do submit to a more general kind of censorship, under which they agree not to print any news at all about certain matters for indefinite periods of time. Sometimes this semicensorship is more or less imposed from without. Sometimes the newspapers and other journalistic media impose it on themselves.

During wartime, for example, newspapers, radio, and television sometimes withhold news for days, weeks, or even months through fear of jeopardizing military operations. And during recent race riots the news media have sometimes delayed or limited their reports through fear of inflaming the passions of both blacks and whites.

This kind of review is beyond the purview of this book. But it does re-emphasize the importance of all of journalism in our society and the heavy responsibility resting on each of its members. And that is really the subject of the next chapter.

9. *The Job Is Yours*

Some years ago two friends of mine were employed by the same magazine. Although it had a sizable staff of editors and writers, it often assigned my friends to the same story. This surprised me because, like other magazines, it usually expected one man to handle any given story by himself.

One day I asked one of my friends the reasons behind the special arrangement. "It's really quite simple," he said. "I ask more and better questions than Pete does. He doesn't have quite enough brass. But he's a better writer. So, when we handle a story together, I ask most of the questions, and he does most of the writing."

It might be nice if more journalistic chores could be handled in this two-platoon fashion, but usually they can't. It might also be nice if journalism required less interviewing, but it doesn't.

To be sure, there are jobs in journalism and allied fields that require little or no interviewing. But these jobs are in the minority, and they are rarely at or near the top of the editorial totem pole. The person who would climb upward on this pole must learn to interview people successfully, if for no other reason than that interviewing is at the very heart of all journalism.

The ability to interview can be cultivated and mastered. No doubt, some men and women are, through inheritance or instinct, better interviewers than others. But whatever gifts they have must be developed. And those who have lesser or seemingly lesser talents can certainly develop those that they have to the fullest. In short, two old clichés do apply: To a considerable degree, interviewers are made, not born. And practice does make perfect.

This book has tried to emphasize a number of qualities and steps essential to good interviewing. Thus it has stressed the importance of being a friendly human being, of showing enterprise in seeking interviews, of preparing in advance of an interview whenever possible, of knowing how to record an interview both by tape and by paper and pencil, of maintaining control of an interview, of listening to the interviewee with uncommon care, and so on. But there are two other qualities that a good journalist often needs if he is to be successful as an interviewer.

One is persistence. Occasionally an interview can be obtained through tactful persistence when all else fails. This is most likely to be the case when a journalist is trying to interview someone of considerable stature.

For example, in 1968 the Columbia Broadcasting System featured what was unquestionably one of the most successful and interesting interviews ever held on television. The interviewers were Martin Agronsky and Eric Sevareid. The interviewee was the late Hugo L. Black, then the aging senior Associate Justice of the U.S. Supreme Court.

Any journalist who had managed to interview Black about anything would have achieved a considerable feat, if only because Supreme Court Justices are notoriously reticent with the press. But to persuade him to appear on an hour-long television show and to discuss some of the Court's most famous and controversial decisions was a real coup. Later Agronsky confessed that it had taken him four years to persuade Black to appear. In short, persistence did pay off.

Nor is this the only example that could be cited of the power of persistence. Barbara Walters of the National Broadcasting Company's *Today* show once pestered former Secretary of State Dean Rusk for nearly two years before he finally agreed to grant her an interview. The resulting dialogue was so extensive that it had to be televised in five parts. Similarly, a reporter for the *New York Times* once badgered Charles A. Lindbergh for six months in order to get to see him. It was the first interview that the famous, but publicity-shy, aviator had given in more than 30 years.

Another quality the good interviewer often needs is imagination. As was suggested in an earlier chapter, it has only been through an imaginative approach to some of today's hippier actors and actresses that some journalists have been able to get them to start talking.

Take another example of imaginative interviewing—one from a newspaper's sports pages. In 1967 and 1968 Yale University boasted one of the Ivy League's all-time great quarterbacks, a young man named Brian Dowling. In 1968 he led his team to a one-sided triumph over Dartmouth in a game that was watched by 50,000 people in person and by many more on television.

Figuring perhaps that many of the people who were interested in the game were already familiar with its highlights, William N. Wallace, a sportswriter for the *New York Times,* devoted only a few sentences to detailing the scoring and the statistics in Sunday's newspaper. Instead, he devoted most of his 25-paragraph story to an interview with Dowling. In the interview the quarterback explained the thinking and action that had gone into seven of the most important offensive plays Yale had made during the game. It was an imaginative kind of story to do under any circumstances and especially so as a replacement for a routine account of how the two teams had trudged up and down the playing field.

Surely it would seem unnecessary to mention that a journalist also has a responsibility to be honest, whether he is interviewing someone or performing some other professional task. But apparently this assumption is not necessarily correct.

A few years ago *Newsweek* reported that the Radio Corporation of America had provided some 1,400 radio stations across the country with taped mock interviews with several prominent entertainers, such as Carol Channing, Duke Ellington, and Henry Fonda. These stars had recorded answers to certain questions. And disk jockeys at the 1,400 radio stations were able to ask and record the questions suggested by these answers. To help the jockeys to do the job right, RCA had provided them with scripts that suggested how to word the questions. In short, the announcers were able to create the illusion that they had actually interviewed the entertainers. Of course, they had really done no such thing.

Disk jockeys are not journalists. They are not even on the fringes of journalism. But the stations that employ them are in the field of journalism if only because they carry news reports. And *Newsweek* reported that an executive with one New England station had openly bragged that many listeners had "swallowed the interview ruse hook, line, and sinker."

Incidents like this should serve as sufficient reminder to any journalist or any person allied to journalism that he has a personal responsibility to maintain the highest standards of integrity in all that he does. Fortunately, there are signs that many journalists take this responsibility seriously.

Early in 1972, the Minnesota Newspaper Association spearheaded a drive that resulted in the formation of the Minnesota Press Council, nine of whose 18 members are nonjournalists. The Council gives residents of the state who believe they have been unfairly or inaccurately portrayed by the press a chance to air their grievances without having to file a libel suit. And reports of its hearings and findings are published in almost all of the newspapers in the state.

For a number of years the Columbia University School of Journalism has published the *Columbia Journalism Review,* a quarterly devoted to reporting and commenting upon the best and worst examples of current journalism. And not long after the close of the 1968 Democratic National Convention several dozen Chicago journalists banded together and, among other things, began publishing the *Chicago Journalism Review.* Angered by what they considered pressure from their own publications to suppress unfavorable convention news about Mayor Richard Daley and Chicago policemen, the journalists determined to improve professional standards and publicly condemn obvious breaches of journalistic ethics.

Since then, similar journals have sprung up in at least a half-dozen American cities, ranging from New York to Honolulu. And the Washington *Post* has even gone so far as to establish an internal ombudsman to review its work and suggest improvements. Says the ombudsman: "We are a big, powerful institution in this society, and we're not perfect. My job is mainly to monitor the newspaper for fairness, balance, and perspective. If I see something wrong and the top editors agree with my criticism, they put out a memo and fix it."

If morality doesn't urge such concern on all journalists, practicality should. Journalism has its enemies. It always will have.

Lately, however, this enmity has sometimes seemed to know no bounds. During the convention cited above, some two score journalists required medical attention. Most of them had been attacked by the police, who seemed particularly interested in preventing photographers and TV cameramen from recording riots that took place and the action the police took against the rioters. A few of these journalists were severely beaten. Although this is the worst incident that comes to mind, it is not the only time in recent years that journalists have been physically attacked while trying to do their jobs.

Usually, of course, enmity against journalists takes a subtler form. Courts, corporations, and government agencies on the federal, state, and local levels deliberately withhold information that would be of benefit to the general public or to certain individual publics to know. Whenever a journalist is barred from seeing official records or from interviewing certain people there is a question as to whether the American people are not the losers, assuming, of course, that national security or some similar good is not involved.

Certainly journalism in general, and newspapers in particular, are in the very front rank of those who can, do, and must protect many of our fundamental freedoms and the nation itself from tyranny, corruption, and dereliction of duty. And certainly the chance to report unfavorable news, without fear or favor, is one of journalism's strongest weapons.

But if journalists are to open all the doors that they should open and receive all the cooperation that they would like, they must do even more than they have done to keep their own house in order. The greatest accomplishments in this area will not come through committees, new and improved codes of ethics, or the commentary of critical journals. The greatest accomplishments will come through the day-in and day-out actions of individual journalists who believe that their calling is high and their responsibility great—to themselves, to their employers, and to their publics. The journalist who is as honest, as fair, and as responsible as he knows how to be will accomplish more than any group within or without the profession.

Consider these words from Walter Lippmann, who was for many years the most distinguished newspaper columnist in this country. In a speech he gave before the National Press Club on his 70th birthday, he said: "If the country is to be governed with the consent of the governed, then the governed must ar-

rive at opinions about what their governors want them to consent to . . . Here we correspondents perform an essential
service. In some field of interest, we make it our business to
find out what is going on under the surface and beyond the
horizon . . .

"In this we do what every sovereign citizen is supposed to
do, but has not the time or the interest to do for himself. This
is our job. It is no mean calling. We have a right to be proud
of it and to be glad that it is our work."

If a clarion call like Lippmann's helps bolster the pride and
dedication of responsible journalists, it is well to remember
that many people do not regard journalism either as important
or as responsible as most journalists themselves regard it. These
people should not necessarily be viewed as enemies of the press.
Indeed, some of them are among the most intelligent and reflective persons in the land.

One is Erik H. Erikson, the famous psychoanalyst who has
won a Pulitzer Prize, a National Book Award, and many other
indications of national and international respect. During nearly
four decades in this country, Erikson adamantly refused to
grant interviews of any kind to journalists.

Then, in late 1970, *Newsweek* published a five-page article
on his influence on psychoanalytic thought. In conjunction with
the article, Erikson agreed to provide written answers to a few
questions that the editors had submitted to him. In one answer
he explained how journalism looks to him:

"I have been wondering why any dialogue with a journalist—
even in writing—seems to me to be such a forbidding business,"
he wrote. "You provide a clue to my dilemma by saying that
journalism is the art of the immediate. I respect this.

"Psychoanalysis, on the other hand, is the art of dealing with
unconscious processes, and that means with the slowest changes
in man. Yet, in the enforced brevity of your contexts, we always

seem to be offering immediate diagnoses of health or sickness, judgments of goodness or badness, or advice on 'how to.'

"Take the 'hot' problem of punitiveness vs. permissiveness in dealing with children. . . . We see the *suppression* of badness in children related to the *repression* of what is unacceptable in ourselves and the *oppression* of people deemed inferior. And we believe that real change in the relation of the generations will come only as alternatives develop in all these—and more—areas. But when we are seduced into trying to state the various alternatives without their complex implications, we foster slogans, soon serving the cheaper kind of journalism—and even cheaper campaign oratory. So we must choose our own daily work of therapy, teaching, and writing as the contexts within which we have sufficient information and enough time to diagnose and to advise."

However pertinent this commentary may be, journalists will, of course, continue to conduct interviews with all kinds of authorities on all kinds of subjects for as far into the future as we can imagine. As this book has suggested again and again, interviewing is the bedrock of journalism. If editors, writers, and reporters had to rely solely on written records and on what they saw with their own eyes—if they could not seek the face-to-face opinions of people, great and small—journalism would not be half so interesting, important, or influential as it is today.

Yet it is well to keep matters in perspective. Interviews can be overdone or wrongly done. They can be held too often. And they can be conducted with the wrong people.

Jack Gould, who was for many years the highly respected television and radio critic of the *New York Times,* brought home this point very vividly in a column he wrote following the 1968 political conventions. Chiding the three major television networks for their coverage of the Democratic convention in particular, he wrote:

"Both the Columbia Broadcasting System . . . and the National Broadcasting Company were so bent on staging their own show that the viewer was deprived of hearing the full range of disagreement over the Vietnamese war plank, to cite only one example. . . . The two chains providing gavel-to-gavel coverage became rattled and relied excessively on their floor reporters, who interviewed and reinterviewed delegates to the exclusion of the business of the convention. . . .

"The networks themselves need to be more careful and restrained. For too many hours at a time the viewer might easily [have decided] that the anchormen and floor reporters [were] the substance of a convention, rather than the delegates and candidates. There is a bolt loose somewhere when the familiar faces of [Walter] Cronkite, [Chet] Huntley and [David] Brinkley, and Howard K. Smith are on camera more than the people ostensibly making the news.

"The whole concept of omnipotent anchormen has had the effect of coming between the viewer and the event in which he is interested. TV's conceit that it is invariably more interesting than what is being said on the podium is simply not true. The viewer has some rights in arriving at these judgments for himself, and the function of TV is then to provide unobtrusive background material."

Thus the wheel comes full circle. Early in this book I indicated that it was important that you impress the people you interview as a decent human being. I also stressed that it was important that you not overemphasize your own role in your interviews and that you put the person you interview and his opinions ahead of your own feelings. If you will do these two things—and if you will master the relatively simple techniques that I have mentioned elsewhere—then, presuming that you have any talent for journalism at all, I do not see how you can fail as an interviewer.

Index